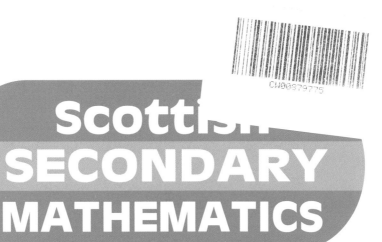

Scottish SECONDARY MATHEMATICS

Tom Sanaghan

Jim Pennel

Carol Munro

Carole Ford

John Dalton

James Cairns

Inspiring generations

Heinemann is an imprint of Pearson Education Limited,
a company incorporated in England and Wales, having
its registered office at Edinburgh Gate Harlow, Essex,
CM20 2JE.

Registered company number: 872828

Heinemann is the registered trademark of
Pearson Education Limited

First published 2004

11 10
10 9 8 7 6 5 4 3 2

British Library Cataloguing in Publication Data is available
from the British Library on request.

ISBN 978 0 435 04013 0

Illustrations by Gustavo Mazali
Cover design by mcc design ltd.
Printed in Malaysia, CTP KHL
Cover photo: © National Museum of Scotland

Acknowledgements
The authors and publishers would also like to thank Alex McKee for assistance with the
manuscript. The authors and publishers would also like to thank the following for
permission to use photographs:

P11: Corbis; P13, P14: Getty Images UK/Photodisk; P16: Alamy Images; P17: Corbis;
P23: Topham Picturepoint; P60: Rex Features; P63: Topham Picturepoint (golden eagle),
Alamy Images (hummingbird), NHPA (magpie and parrot), Getty Images UK/Taxi
(swan); P74: Getty Images UK/Photodisk, P79: Getty Images UK/Photodisk (left); Getty
Images UK/Stone (right); P84: Topham Picturepoint; P86: Topham Picturepoint; P92:
Getty Images UK/Photodisk; P93: Topham Picturepoint; P119: Getty Images UK/Photodisk;
P127: Harcourt Education Ltd/Peter Evans; P128: Getty Images UK/Photodisk.

Contents

How to use this book

Every chapter is divided into sections.
Each section begins with a list of key points:

1.1 Rounding

Our numbers were developed from the Arabic system giving the digits 0–9.

An exercise follows:

Exercise 1.1

1 Round the following numbers to the nearest: **(i)** ten   **(ii)** hundred   **(iii)** thousand
   (a) 6172   **(b)** 18 776   **(c)** 5217

At the end of the chapter is a review exercise and a summary of all the key points.

Special instructions are shown by these symbols:

W   You need to use the matching numbered worksheet to answer this question.

Use a calculator to answer these questions.

1 Whole numbers

In this chapter you will extend your knowledge of working with whole numbers.

1.1 Reading numbers

All numbers can be made up using the digits 0, 1, 2, 3, 4, 5, 6, 7, 8, 9. The place of the digits tells us about the size of the number.

Numbers can be written using words or figures.

Th	H	T	U	
	8	0	4	eight hundred and four
2	0	2	6	two thousand and twenty six
3	0	0	5	three thousand and five
5	2	0	3	five thousand two hundred and three

In the number 5203

- the 5 stands for 5 thousands
- the 2 stands for 2 hundreds
- the 0 stands for 0 tens
- the 3 stands for 3 units

Example

Write the number which is:

(**a**) 70 more than 410

```
  H T U
  4 1 0
+   7 0
_____
  4 8 0
```

(**b**) 200 less than 6500

```
  Th H T U
   6 5 0 0
 −   2 0 0
_____
   6 3 0 0
```

Make sure the columns are lined up correctly

Exercise 1.1

You need Worksheet **1.1** for question **1**.

2 Write the following numbers using figures:
  (**a**) thirty two
  (**b**) two hundred and seventeen
  (**c**) six hundred and four
  (**d**) four hundred and ten
  (**e**) five thousand, one hundred and twenty three
  (**f**) six thousand and seventeen
  (**g**) two thousand and eight.

> **Heinemann Bank**
> 10-20-30
> Date _30-6-04_
> Pay _Mrs Macsporran_
> _Four pounds and_   £ _4.55_
> _fifty-five pence_
> Signature _Bruce Robertson_

3 Write the following numbers in words:
  (**a**) 43   (**b**) 90   (**c**) 714   (**d**) 825
  (**e**) 570   (**f**) 305   (**g**) 2174   (**h**) 2006
  (**i**) 6050   (**j**) 3200   (**k**) 1999   (**l**) 8054

4 What does the digit 2 stand for in each of these numbers?
  (**a**) 25   (**a**) 2039   (**c**) 270   (**d**) 652

5 (**a**) Using the digits 3, 1, 7 and 9, what is the largest and smallest four digit number you can make?
  (**b**) Choose four different digits and write the largest and smallest number you can make using all of them.

  3 1 7 9

6 Write the number which is:
  (**a**) 100 more than 340   (**b**) 20 less than 670
  (**c**) 500 less than 824   (**d**) 30 more than 2761
  (**e**) 7000 more than 2160   (**f**) 400 less than 5800

7 Using figures, write any number that has:
  (**a**) a 5 in the hundreds column
  (**b**) an 8 in the thousands column and a 0 in the tens column
  (**c**) a 9 in the thousands column, a 1 in the hundreds column and a number less than 6 in the units column
  (**d**) a number less than 5 in the thousands column
  (**e**) a digit in the hundreds column which is less than the digit in the tens column.

8 A game for two players.
You need Worksheet **1.2**, a calculator and scissors.

Rules

Cut along the dotted lines so that each player has three cards.

Player 1

• Read out the four numbers on one of your cards to Player 2.

Player 2

• Write down the four numbers.
• Add them up using a calculator.
• Compare your answer with Player 1's answers.
• If your answers agree with Player 1's, then you score 2 points.
  If not, check your answers with Player 1 to find out why you were wrong.

Player 2 should now read out the four numbers on one of their cards
and repeat the above.
Repeat until both players have used all three cards.

9 A game for any number of players. You need Worksheet **1.3** and scissors.
Each player will need a set of 0–9 cards cut from Worksheet **1.3**.

Rules

Collect all the cards and shuffle them. Deal ten cards to each player.

Round one

• Everyone puts down one card (face down).
• Turn the cards over. The highest card gets one point.
• Put these cards to one side. They cannot be used again in this game.

Round two

• Everyone puts down two cards to make a two digit number (face down).
• Turn the cards over. The highest number gets two points.
• Put these cards to one side. They cannot be used again in this game.

Round three

• Repeat for three cards to make a three digit number.
• The winner gets three points.

Round four

• Repeat for four cards to make a four digit number.
• The winner gets four points.

Reshuffle all the cards and play again. The first person to get 20 points
wins the game.

1.2 Ordering numbers

Example   Put the following numbers in order:

642, 729, 632, 606, 709, 600

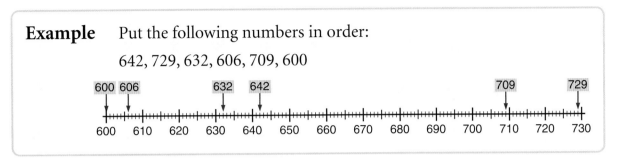

Exercise 1.2

You need Worksheets **1.4** and **1.5** for questions **1** and **2**.
You also need scissors.

W 3 Find the missing numbers **a** to **h** on these number lines.

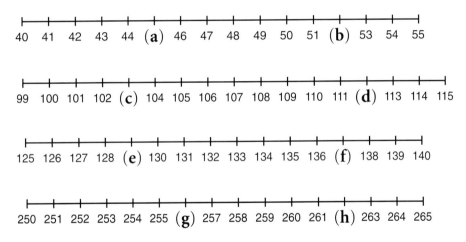

4 Write the following numbers in order.
Start with the smallest.

(**a**) 34, 76, 12, 32, 9, 66

(**b**) 17, 38, 29, 18, 30, 26

(**c**) 40, 38, 45, 52, 47, 46

(**d**) 87, 95, 108, 99, 89, 103

(**e**) 162, 109, 130, 146, 190, 129

(**f**) 172, 148, 190, 109, 127, 174

(**g**) 725, 710, 704, 762, 718, 764

(**h**) 1055, 930, 1627, 1422, 1529, 1657

5 Starting with the smallest, list these pupils in order of height.

Name	Alice	Ben	Callum	Denise	Elliot	Fran	Gina
Height (cm)	133	176	124	143	108	164	118

6 Write these rivers in order from shortest to longest.

River	Congo	Mackenzie	Nile	Amur	Amazon	Lena
Length (km)	4667	4241	6650	4509	6437	4270

1.3 Rounding to the nearest ten

Sometimes an exact answer is not needed.
You can give an **approximate** answer by rounding.

Examples (a) Round 46 to the nearest 10.

46 is closer to 50 than 40

46 is **50** rounded to the nearest ten.

(b) Round 382 to the nearest ten.

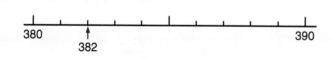

382 is closer to 380 than 390

382 is **380** rounded to the nearest ten.

Exercise 1.3

W You need Worksheet **1.6** for question **1**.

2 Round each number to the nearest ten.

(**a**) 63   (**b**) 48   (**c**) 77   (**d**) 43   (**e**) 31

(**f**) 6   (**g**) 18   (**h**) 65   (**i**) 34   (**j**) 35

(**k**) 9   (**l**) 29   (**m**) 51   (**n**) 99   (**o**) 3

3 Round each number to the nearest ten.

(**a**) 152   (**b**) 236   (**c**) 149   (**d**) 365

(**e**) 288   (**f**) 523   (**g**) 578   (**h**) 297

(**i**) 692   (**j**) 741   (**k**) 377   (**l**) 998

4 Round each height to the nearest ten metres.

Waterfall	Height (m)
Niagara	54
Angel	979
Tugela	948
Yosemite	739
Sutherland	580
Kjellfossen	561

You need Worksheets **1.7** and **1.8**, scissors and a calculator for question **5**.
You need Worksheet **1.9** for questions **6** and **7**.

1.4 Addition

How many pairs of shoes are there in Hilda's shop?

I've counted 153 pairs.

I've counted 79 pairs.

I've counted 36 pairs.

That's 268 pairs of shoes all together.

153
79
36
268

Remember to check that your answer is sensible.

The sum of 153, 79 and 36 is 268.

Exercise 1.4

W You need Worksheet **1.10** for question **1**.

2 Calculate:

(**a**) 46 + 23   (**b**) 32 + 19   (**c**) 25 + 16

(**d**) 73 + 9   (**e**) 90 + 50   (**f**) 70 + 89

(**g**) 186 + 32   (**h**) 185 + 46   (**i**) 207 + 85

3 Ruth wants to buy a pair of jeans for £49 and a top for £12.
How much will this cost her?

4 Mrs Muir, the librarian, buys two books costing £15 and £36.
What is the total cost of the books?

5 Dylan cycled the following route while on holiday:

Friday   Templeton to Rigby
Saturday   Rigby to Masefield
Sunday   Masefield to Darville

How far did he cycle altogether?

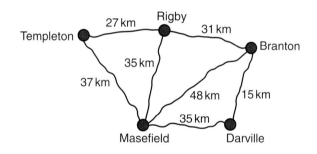

6 The Welton family pays 3 bills: Gas   –   £83
                             Telephone – £131
                             Electricity –   £78

How much did they pay in total?

7 Lindsay is buying a present for her gran.
She wants to buy 3 items and spend no more than £16.

(**a**) Can she afford to buy the hand cream, soap and
shower gel?

(**b**) Can she afford to buy the perfume, hand cream
and soap?

W (**c**) On Worksheet **1.10**, list 5 other ways Lindsay
could spend her money.

Kells of Kirkaldy	
Soap	£3
Shower gel	£8
Bath oil	£8
Body Spray	£4
Hand cream	£5
Perfume	£9

1.5 Subtraction

Exercise 1.5

W You need Worksheet **1.11** for question **1**.

2 Calculate:

(**a**) 82 − 24   (**b**) 87 − 38   (**c**) 74 − 6

(**d**) 60 − 25   (**e**) 142 − 60   (**f**) 725 − 9

(**g**) 365 − 83   (**h**) 231 − 52   (**i**) 310 − 27

3 Alice threw a 6 and landed on square 32 of her snakes and ladders board.
On which square was her counter before this move?

4 The temperature in Edinburgh was 21°C and the temperature in Aviemore was 9°C.
Find the difference between these temperatures.

5 Vicky has managed to save £700. If she spends £339 on a holiday, how much will she have left?

6 Peter was 106 centimetres tall when he was six.
By the time he was sixteen he was 192 centimetres.
By how much had he grown?

7 There were 129 people on a trip to Edinburgh.
52 people stayed in the town centre, 36 went to Holyrood Palace and the rest went to visit Ocean Terminal Shopping Centre.
How many people went to Ocean Terminal?

1.6 Multiplication

Exercise 1.6

W You may use the tables square on Worksheet **1.11** for these questions.

W You need Worksheet **1.12** for question **1**.

2 Find:
   (**a**) 3×7 (**b**) 5×3 (**c**) 4×6
   (**d**) 7×3 (**e**) 6×8 (**f**) 9×4
   (**g**) 9×8 (**h**) 6×7 (**i**) 4×8

3 Find:
   (**a**) 10×6 (**b**) 14×5 (**c**) 23×7
   (**d**) 62×8 (**e**) 44×4 (**f**) 21×1
   (**g**) 37×3 (**h**) 57×9 (**i**) 83×9

4 A packet of Mintees costs 14 pence.
   How much will 8 packets cost?

5 Mouser the cat eats 55 grams of cat biscuits every day.
   How much will she eat in seven days?

6 Golders fruit company pack apples in boxes of 24.
   How many apples will be in six boxes?

7 Angela can deliver newspapers to 95 houses in 1 hour.
   How many houses will she deliver to in 3 hours?

1.7 Multiplying by ten

To multiply a number by 10 you move every digit one place to the left.

Examples

(a)

(b)

Exercise 1.7

1 Find:

(a) 7×10 (b) 9×10 (c) 10×10

(d) 10×24 (e) 76×10 (f) 38×10

(g) 75×10 (h) 10×49 (i) 125×10

(j) 10×136 (k) 482×10 (l) 201×10

2 Gloria is collecting money for charity.
If she collects £10 each from 6 people, how much does she collect together?

3 A packet of sweets costs 15 pence.
What is the cost of 10 packets?

4 A lorry holds 765 pipes.
If each pipe weighs 10 kilograms, what weight does
the lorry hold?

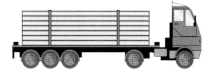

5 Ali has 324 marbles.
Each marble weighs 10 g.
What is the total weight of the marbles?

6 Jeff sells books of raffle tickets.
Each book contains 10 tickets.
He sells 102 books.
How many tickets does Jeff sell?

1.8 Division

112 packs of sweets have to be divided among 8 bags.

14 packs per bag

Exercise 1.8

W You need Worksheets **1.13** and **1.14** for question **1**.

2 Calculate:
   (a) $16 \div 4$ (b) $32 \div 2$ (c) $27 \div 9$
   (d) $56 \div 8$ (e) $49 \div 7$ (f) $60 \div 10$
   (g) $54 \div 6$ (h) $35 \div 5$ (i) $72 \div 9$

W You need Worksheet **1.15** for question **3**.

4 Calculate:
   (a) $84 \div 3$ (b) $36 \div 2$ (c) $85 \div 5$
   (d) $56 \div 4$ (e) $91 \div 7$ (f) $104 \div 8$
   (g) $132 \div 6$ (h) $132 \div 4$ (i) $108 \div 9$

5 Mr Arnold has 32 coloured pencils. He shares them equally among 4 pupils.
How many pencils does each pupil receive?

6 David, Anna and Catherine share £60 equally among themselves.
How much is each share?

7 Melvin's Store sells packs of 6 pens for 42 pence.
How much is one pen?

8 Barry's lamp changes colour 5 times every 60 minutes.
How long does it stay on each colour?

9 Martin uses 120 grams of flour to make 8 biscuits.
How much flour does each biscuit need?

10 Rupa has 68 metres of material. If it takes 4 metres of
material to make a dress, how many dresses can she make?

11 Find the smallest number that can be divided by:
(**a**) 4 and 5   (**b**) 3 and 7   (**c**) 4 and 6

You need Worksheet **1.15** for questions **12** and **13**.

1.9 Dividing by ten

To divide a number by 10, move every digit one place to the right.

Example 1   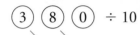

Example 2   

Exercise 1.9

1 Find:
(**a**) 160 ÷ 10   (**b**) 820 ÷ 10   (**c**) 540 ÷ 10
(**d**) 260 ÷ 10   (**e**) 470 ÷ 10   (**f**) 600 ÷ 10
(**g**) 500 ÷ 10   (**h**) 900 ÷ 10   (**i**) 720 ÷ 10

2 A £450 prize is to be shared among 10 people.
How much will each person receive?

3 A 350 centimetre ribbon is to be cut into 10 centimetre strips.
How many strips can be cut?

4 630 people are invited to a charity dinner.
If 10 people are seated at each table, how many tables will be needed?

1.10 Solving number problems

Step 1 – Read the question.

Step 2 – Find the important information.

Step 3 – Decide how to solve the problem.

Step 4 – Calculate the answer.

Example 1

Greta collects charity money boxes.
One morning she collected three boxes.

Box 1 – £52   Box 2 – £68   Box 3 – £34

How much did she collect in total?

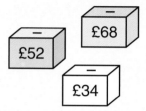

$$
\begin{array}{r}
£52 \\
£68 \\
+ \ £34 \\
\hline
£154
\end{array}
$$

Total means add

£154 **She collected £154.**

Example 2

Pete has to drive 98 miles.
He wants to take a break so he splits the
journey into 2 equal parts.
How long is each part?

To split something
means divide

Aberdeen
98 miles

$$
\begin{array}{r}
49 \\
2\overline{)98}
\end{array}
$$ **Each part is 49 miles long.**

Exercise 1.10

1 Lena, Megan and Anne are going on holiday to Italy.
They each paid £179.
What was the total cost of the holiday?

2 Norway have won 260 Winter Olympic medals and
Canada have won 95.
How many more medals have Norway won?

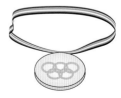

3 Laura's dress was 172 centimetres long.
She had it shortened by 15 centimetres.
What length is it now?

4 The number 38 bus from Stirling to Edinburgh picked up
24 passengers in Stirling and 12 passengers in Kirkliston.
If 18 passengers left the bus at Newbridge, how many
passengers were left in the bus?

5 Beryl buys 8 chairs costing £65 each.
What was the total cost of the chairs?

6 A lottery syndicate of 6 people won £192.
How much would they each receive if they shared the
money equally?

7 In a competition Jack won £300.
He spent £238 on a new television and shared
the rest equally between his two children.
How much did each child receive?

8 The pupils in class 1X2 are weighed.

Claire – 35 kg	Thomas – 39 kg	Leah– 42 kg
Jed – 42 kg	Nirma – 40 kg	Robbie – 48 kg
Aisha – 38 kg	Morven – 44 kg	Duncan – 47 kg
Gordon – 40 kg	Angus – 50 kg	Leslie – 38 kg

(**a**) What is the difference in weight between the heaviest and
lightest person?

(**b**) What is the total weight of Claire, Leah and Thomas?

(**c**) 3 pupils are needed to help with lighting in the school hall.
Their total weight should be less than 120 kg.

Copy and complete the table to show 5 different combinations
of pupils who could be chosen.

pupil 1	pupil 2	pupil 3	total weight (kg)
Claire	Nirma	Morven	35 + 40 + 44 = 119

1.11 Mental calculations

Method 1

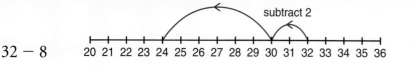

$14 + 8$ The answer is 22.

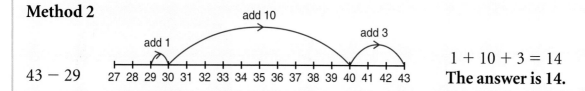

$32 - 8$ The answer is 24.

Method 2

$43 - 29$

$1 + 10 + 3 = 14$
The answer is 14.

Exercise 1.11

1 Calculate mentally:

(**a**) $30 + 7$ (**b**) $40 + 2$ (**c**) $20 + 9$

(**d**) $20 - 5$ (**e**) $40 - 3$ (**f**) $30 - 7$

(**g**) $70 - 8$ (**h**) $60 - 9$ (**i**) $50 - 4$

2 Use method 1 to find:

(**a**) $15 + 6$ (**b**) $24 + 8$ (**c**) $19 + 4$ (**d**) $13 + 9$

(**e**) $317 + 5$ (**f**) $237 + 6$ (**g**) $15 - 6$ (**h**) $32 - 7$

(**i**) $146 - 8$ (**j**) $151 - 7$ (**k**) $122 - 9$ (**l**) $234 - 7$

3 Find mentally:

(**a**) $40 + 20$ (**b**) $50 + 40$ (**c**) $70 + 30$

(**d**) $70 + 40$ (**e**) $80 + 60$ (**f**) $120 + 30$

(**g**) $150 + 50$ (**h**) $170 + 50$ (**i**) $130 + 80$

(**j**) $180 - 70$ (**k**) $120 - 30$ (**l**) $200 - 60$

(**m**) $90 - 90$ (**n**) $120 - 40$ (**o**) $110 - 50$

(**p**) $210 - 50$ (**q**) $250 - 100$ (**r**) $150 - 80$

4 Use method 2 to find:

(**a**) $90 - 76$ (**b**) $40 - 17$ (**c**) $80 - 37$

(**d**) $31 - 24$ (**e**) $44 - 39$ (**f**) $45 - 29$

(**g**) $82 - 69$ (**h**) $34 - 26$ (**i**) $36 - 27$

1.12 Sequences

A sequence is a special list of numbers.
2, 4, 6, 8, 10, 12, 14 16 …
3, 6, 9, 12, 15, 18, 21 …

Sometimes a rule can be found to continue a sequence.

Sequence   **Rule**
3, 7, 11, 15, 19, 23 …   Add 4 to find the next number.

Exercise 1.12

W You need Worksheet **1.16** for questions **1** and **2**.

3 Copy and complete:

(**a**) 5, 10, 15, 20, 25, 30, __, __   (**b**) 4, 6, 8, 10, __, __

(**c**) 6, 10, 14, 18, 22, __, __   (**d**) 24, 20, 16, 12, __, __

(**e**) 42, 36, 30, 24, 18, __, __   (**f**) 20, 17, 14, 11, __, __

4 Write the next two numbers and the rule for each sequence.

(**a**) 1, 3, 5, 7   (**b**) 4, 10, 16, 22   (**c**) 11, 23, 35, 47

(**d**) 40, 32, 24, 16   (**e**) 10, 19, 28, 37   (**f**) 100, 80, 60, 40

5 The sequence of numbers 0, 2, 4, 6, 8, 10, 12, … is called **even numbers**.

The sequence of numbers 1, 3, 5, 7, 9, 11, … is called **odd numbers**.

68	213	92	9	914
12	11	104	26	327
638	40		261	
1007		17		8

(**a**) List the numbers above which are odd.

(**b**) List the numbers above which are even.

6 Write the first ten numbers in the sequence which:

(**a**) starts at 5 and increases by 2

(**b**) starts at 7 and increases by 5

7 Jane bought a tree which was 15 centimetres high.
It grew 3 centimetres every month.
How high was it after 4 months?

1.13 Number puzzles

Exercise 1.13

1 Copy and complete these calculations:

(**a**) $4 + \square = 9$

(**b**) $15 \;\square\; 3 = 12$

(**c**) $17 - \square = 11$

(**d**) $15 - \square = 10$

(**e**) $4 \times \square = 24$

(**f**) $7 \times \square = 56$

(**g**) $9 \times \square = 27$

(**h**) $10 \;\square\; 6 = 60$

(**i**) $50 \div \square = 10$

(**j**) $42 \div \square = 6$

(**k**) $36 \;\square\; 6 = 6$

(**l**) $4 \times \square = 16$

(**m**) $17 + \square = 21$

(**n**) $35 \;\square\; 17 = 18$

2 Find two ways of completing each of these calculations:

(**a**) $5 \;\square\;\square = 25$

(**b**) $6 \;\square\;\square = 2$

$5 \;\square\;\square = 25$

$6 \;\square\;\square = 2$

W You need Worksheet **1.17** for question **3**.
The eleven pieces can be joined together to make
a 100 square.
Write the missing numbers in the empty squares,
then cut out the pieces and stick them into your
jotter to make a 100 square.

1	2	3	4	5	6	7	8	9	10
11	12	13	14	15	16	17	18	19	20
21	22	23	24	25	26	27	28		
31	32	33	34	35	36				
41	42	43	44	45					
51	52								
61									

Review exercise 1

1 Write the following numbers using figures:

   (**a**) two hundred and eighty

   (**b**) six hundred and four

   (**c**) four thousand one hundred and six

   (**d**) eight thousand and fifty.

2 Write the following numbers in order, starting with the smallest.

   (**a**) 36, 58, 32, 60, 49, 51

   (**b**) 268, 271, 245, 290, 270, 208

   (**c**) 1450, 1335, 1280, 1356, 1309, 1411

4 Round the following numbers to the nearest ten:

   (**a**) 47   (**b**) 82   (**c**) 45   (**d**) 152

   (**e**) 129   (**f**) 206   (**g**) 165   (**h**) 197

4 On Saturday Alice delivered 156 newspapers.
   On Sunday she delivered 85.
   How many did she deliver altogether that weekend?

5 There were 115 people on a train from Glasgow
   to Edinburgh.
   If 67 people left the train at Falkirk, how many
   stayed on the train?

6 Hussein bought 6 rulers for 84 pence.
   How much did each ruler cost?

7 Yvonne's new tyres cost £38 each.
   How much did it cost for 4 tyres?

8 Write the next two numbers and the rule for each sequence.

   (**a**) 4, 7, 10, 13   (**b**) 5, 10, 15, 20

   (**c**) 15, 13, 11, 9   (**d**) 52, 56, 60, 64

Summary

Reading numbers

In the number 3048:
- the 3 stands for 3 thousands
- the 0 stands for 0 hundreds
- the 4 stands for 4 tens
- the 8 stands for 8 units

Rounding

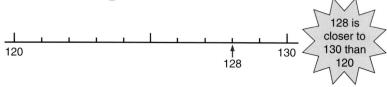

128 is **130** rounded to the nearest ten.

Multiplying and dividing by ten

To multiply by 10, move every digit one place to the left.

To divide by 10, move every digit one place to the right.

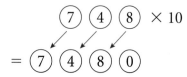

Solving number problems

When attempting a problem:

Step 1 – Read the question.

Step 2 – Find the important information.

Step 3 – Decide how to solve the problem.

Step 4 – Find the answer.

Mental methods

Method 1

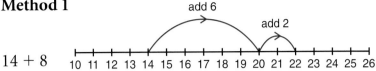

$14 + 8$ **The answer is 22.**

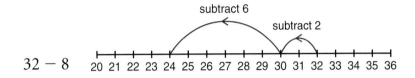

$32 - 8$ **The answer is 24.**

Method 2

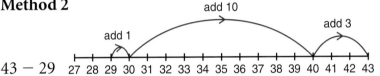

$29 + 1 + 10 + 3 = 43$
The answer is 14.

$43 - 29$

Sequences

A sequence is a special list of numbers.
$2, 4, 6, 8, 10, 12, 14, 16 \ldots$
$3, 6, 9, 12, 15, 18, 21 \ldots$

Sometimes a rule can be found to continue a sequence.

Sequence   Rule
$3, 7, 11, 15, 19, 23 \ldots$ Add 4 to find the next number.

2 Symmetry

In this chapter you will learn about lines of symmetry and symmetrical shapes.

2.1 Lines of symmetry

The dotted line which cuts this shape in half so that one half can be folded exactly onto the other is called a **line of symmetry**.

Some shapes have more than one line of symmetry.

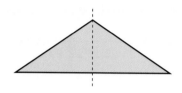

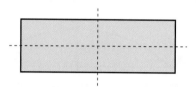

Exercise 2.1

W You need Worksheets **2.1**, **2.2** and **2.3** for questions **1**, **2** and **3**.

4 How many lines of symmetry could you draw on each diagram?

(**a**) 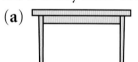 (**b**) (**c**)  (**d**)

5 Copy each shape and draw any lines of symmetry.

(**a**) 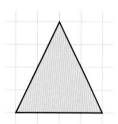 (**b**) 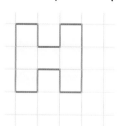 (**c**)

(**d**) 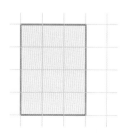 (**e**) 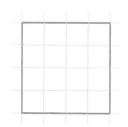 (**f**)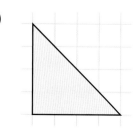

2.2 Symmetrical shapes

A shape which has a line of symmetry is called **symmetrical**.
A mirror may be used to find symmetrical shapes.

Example
Which shapes are symmetrical?

(**a**)

(**b**)

(**c**)

Yes   **No**   **Yes**

Exercise 2.2

W You may use a mirror for this exercise.
You need Worksheet **2.4** for questions **1** to **12**.

13 Which of these are symmetrical?

(**a**)

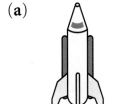

(**b**)

(**c**)

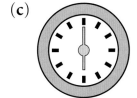

(**d**)

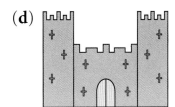

2.3 Reflection

If you place a mirror on a line of symmetry you can see the full shape.

This is called **reflection**.

Reflection may be used to complete the missing half of a symmetrical shape.

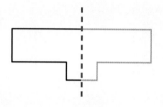

Exercise 2.3

W You need Worksheets **2.5** and **2.6** for questions **1**, **2** and **3**.

4 Copy and complete these shapes using reflection:

(a)

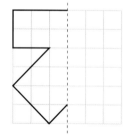

(b)

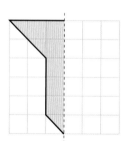

(c)

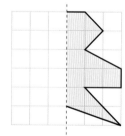

(d)

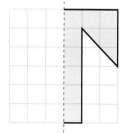

(e)

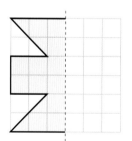

(f)

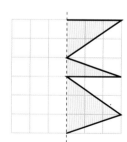

(g)

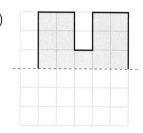

(h)

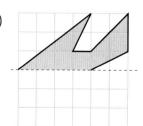

(i)

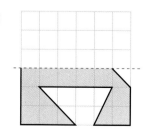

Review exercise 2

1 Which of these pictures are symmetrical?

(a)   (b) 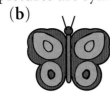   (c) 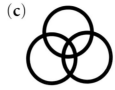   (d)    (e)

2 How many lines of symmetry could you draw on each diagram?

(a) 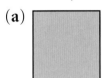   (b) 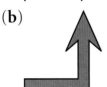   (c) 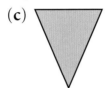   (d)   (e)

3 Copy each shape and draw any lines of symmetry.

(a) 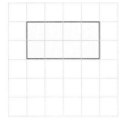   (b) 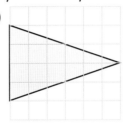   (c)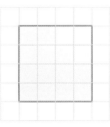

(d) 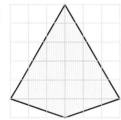   (e) 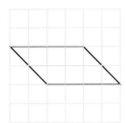   (f)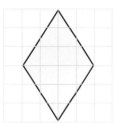

4 Copy and complete the shapes for each line of symmetry.

(a) 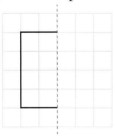   (b) 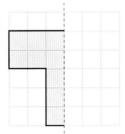   (c)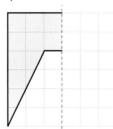

(d) 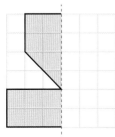   (e) 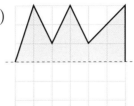   (f)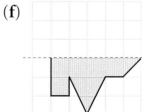

Summary

Symmetry

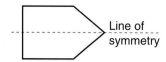

Some shapes can have more than one line of symmetry.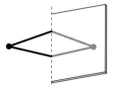

Reflection

Reflection may be used to complete the missing half of a symmetrical shape.

3 Fractions

In this chapter you will learn more about fractions and calculate fractions of quantities.

3.1 Understanding fractions

This pie is divided into **2** equal pieces. Each piece is $\frac{1}{2}$ of the pie.

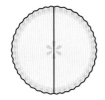

This pizza is divided into **4** equal pieces. Each piece is $\frac{1}{4}$ of the pizza.

Exercise 3.1

What fraction is each piece?

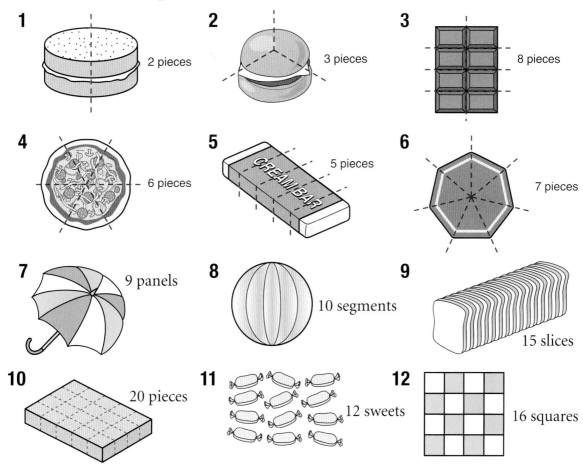

1 2 pieces

2 3 pieces

3 8 pieces

4 6 pieces

5 5 pieces

6 7 pieces

7 9 panels

8 10 segments

9 15 slices

10 20 pieces

11 12 sweets

12 16 squares

W You need Worksheet **3.1** for questions **13** and **14**.

3.2 Further fractions

Example

This pendant has 7 equal parts.
Find the fraction coloured red.

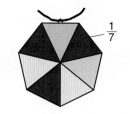

Each red part is $\frac{1}{7}$ of the pendant.
So $\frac{3}{7}$ of the pendant is red and $\frac{4}{7}$ of the pendant is not red.

Exercise 3.2

1 Each pendant has a number of equal parts. Find the fraction coloured red.

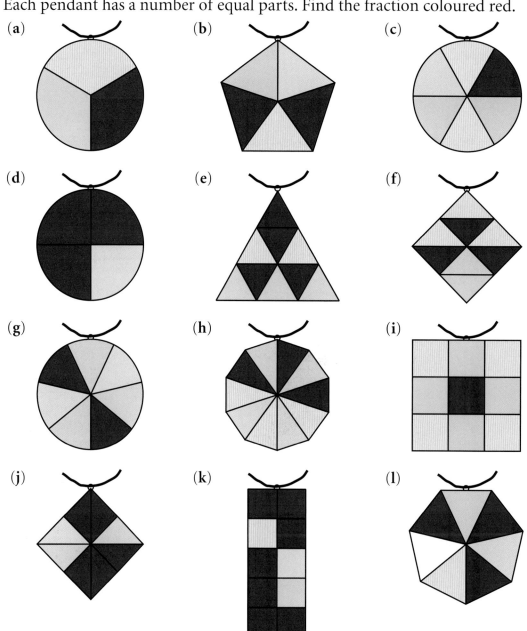

(a)   (b)   (c)

(d)   (e)   (f)

(g)   (h)   (i)

(j)   (k)   (l)

2 For each place mat, write the fraction coloured green.

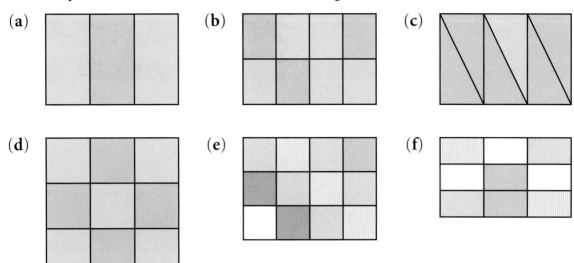

(a) (b) (c)

(d) (e) (f)

3 For each place mat in question 2, write the fraction coloured blue.

W You need Worksheets **3.2** and **3.3** for question **4**.

5 For each group, write the fraction which is (**i**) green (**ii**) not green.

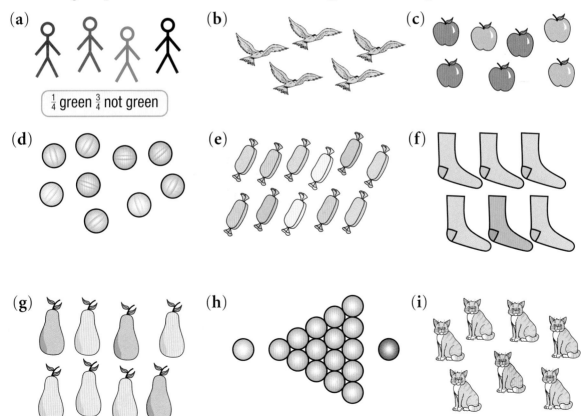

(a) $\frac{1}{4}$ green $\frac{3}{4}$ not green

(b)

(c)

(d)

(e)

(f)

(g)

(h)

(i)

6 Here are 11 animals.
What fraction of the animals are:
  (**i**) horses
  (**ii**) dogs
  (**iii**) hens?

7 This stained glass window has 25 small panes.
What fraction of the window is:
(**a**) red   (**b**) green
(**c**) blue   (**d**) orange?

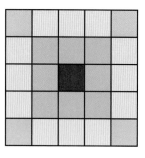

8 Fiona spent 90p in Mrs MacSporran's sweet shop.
What fraction did she spend on:
(**a**) crisps
(**b**) the snacker bar
(**c**) the lollipop
(**d**) the Jelly Beans?

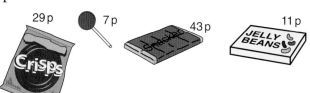

29p   7p   43p   11p

9 What fraction of this group of boys:
  (**i**) is aged 12
  (**ii**) has a name starting with A
  (**iii**) has red hair
  (**iv**) wears glasses
  (**v**) has a name with 3 letters?

John 14   Bill 13   Jim 13   Joe 12
Asif 13   Andy 12   Ahmed 14

10 (**a**) For each strip, write the fraction coloured red.
(**b**) Which is the bigger fraction, $\frac{1}{6}$ or $\frac{1}{8}$?

11 (**a**) For each strip, write the fraction coloured blue.
(**b**) Which is the bigger fraction, $\frac{1}{7}$ or $\frac{1}{9}$?

12 Which is bigger, $\frac{1}{2}$ a pizza or $\frac{1}{5}$ of a pizza?

13 Which group has more children, $\frac{1}{4}$ of the class or $\frac{1}{7}$ of the class?

14 Write these fractions in order, starting with the smallest.

$$\frac{1}{3}, \quad \frac{1}{6}, \quad \frac{1}{2}, \quad \frac{1}{4}, \quad \frac{1}{5},$$

> The bigger the number on the bottom, the smaller the fraction.

3.3 Half of a quantity

To find half of a quantity, divide by 2.

Example 1
Jim and John are each to have **half** of the sweets in this packet.
There are 8 sweets in the packet.
They divide them into two equal amounts.

Jim's sweets   John's sweets

So $\frac{1}{2}$ of $8 = 8 \div 2 = 4$

Example 2
Calculate $\frac{1}{2}$ of £4.28

$\frac{1}{2}$ of £4.28 $=$ £4.28 $\div$ 2
$\qquad = $ **£2.14**

$$\begin{array}{r} 2{\cdot}14 \\ 2\overline{)4{\cdot}28} \end{array}$$

Exercise 3.3

1 Find half of each quantity:

(**a**)

4 bananas

(**b**)

6 apples

(**c**)

10 cakes

(**d**)

12 sweets

(**e**)

14 eggs

(**f**)

20 mints

2 Calculate:

(**a**) $\frac{1}{2}$ of £18 (**b**) $\frac{1}{2}$ of 16 kg (**c**) $\frac{1}{2}$ of 24 m (**d**) $\frac{1}{2}$ of 30 km

(**e**) $\frac{1}{2}$ of 40 pence (**f**) $\frac{1}{2}$ of 100 miles (**g**) $\frac{1}{2}$ of 44 g (**h**) $\frac{1}{2}$ of £36

(**i**) $\frac{1}{2}$ of £6·30 (**j**) $\frac{1}{2}$ of 58 litres (**k**) $\frac{1}{2}$ of 140 mm (**l**) $\frac{1}{2}$ of 250 g

3 Calculate:

(a) $\frac{1}{2}$ of 26 g (b) $\frac{1}{2}$ of £84 (c) $\frac{1}{2}$ of 56 kg (d) $\frac{1}{2}$ of 72 m

(e) $\frac{1}{2}$ of 144 cm (f) $\frac{1}{2}$ of 500 litres (g) $\frac{1}{2}$ of £448 (h) $\frac{1}{2}$ of 126 ml

(i) $\frac{1}{2}$ of 642 miles (j) $\frac{1}{2}$ of 458 mm (k) $\frac{1}{2}$ of £704 (l) $\frac{1}{2}$ of 736 km

4 A carton of orange juice has 280 millilitres and the twins are to have half each. How much will each receive?

5 The bill in the café came to £3.62, and Jill and Amy split it between them. How much did each pay?

6 Half the pupils in first year own a computer. 90 pupils own a computer. How many pupils are there in first year?

3.4 Fractions of a quantity

To find a fraction of a quantity, divide by the number on the bottom of the fraction.

To find $\frac{1}{3}$ divide by 3

To find $\frac{1}{4}$ divide by 4

To find $\frac{1}{8}$ divide by 8

To find $\frac{1}{10}$ divide by 10

Example 1

Calculate $\frac{1}{5}$ of 45 kg

$\frac{1}{5}$ of 45 = 45 ÷ 5

$= 9$

So $\frac{1}{5}$ of 45 kg = 9 kg

Example 2

In a class of 30 pupils $\frac{1}{6}$ of them wear glasses. How many pupils is this?

$\frac{1}{6}$ of 30 = 30 ÷ 6

$= 5$

So 5 of the pupils wear glasses.

Exercise 3.4

1 Calculate $\frac{1}{3}$ of each quantity: (Divide by 3)

(a) 6 miles (b) 3 cm (c) 9 km (d) 12 mm

(e) 21 kg (f) 15 litres (g) 18 ml (h) 30 g

2 Calculate $\frac{1}{4}$ of each quantity: (Divide by 4)

(a) 4 km (b) 12 m (c) 16 mm (d) 20 cm

(e) 28 litres (f) 40 ml (g) 32 kg (h) 36 g

3 Calculate:

(**a**) $\frac{1}{3}$ of £12   (**b**) $\frac{1}{3}$ of 45 kg   (**c**) $\frac{1}{3}$ of 51 g

(**d**) $\frac{1}{5}$ of 40 cm   (**e**) $\frac{1}{5}$ of £100   (**f**) $\frac{1}{5}$ of 25 km

(**g**) $\frac{1}{7}$ of £140   (**h**) $\frac{1}{7}$ of 35 m   (**i**) $\frac{1}{7}$ of 63 litres

(**j**) $\frac{1}{9}$ of 90 tonnes   (**k**) $\frac{1}{9}$ of 54 mm   (**l**) $\frac{1}{9}$ of 360°

4 Find:

(**a**) $\frac{1}{10}$ of 50   (**b**) $\frac{1}{10}$ of 120   (**c**) $\frac{1}{3}$ of 18   (**d**) $\frac{1}{4}$ of 20

(**e**) $\frac{1}{8}$ of 56   (**f**) $\frac{1}{6}$ of 48   (**g**) $\frac{1}{5}$ of 35   (**h**) $\frac{1}{7}$ of 28

(**i**) $\frac{1}{9}$ of 54   (**j**) $\frac{1}{5}$ of 40   (**k**) $\frac{1}{8}$ of 72   (**l**) $\frac{1}{9}$ of 81

W You need Worksheet **3.4** for question **5**.

Review exercise 3

1 What fraction is each piece?

(**a**) 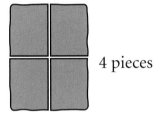 4 pieces

(**b**) 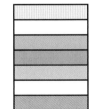 7 stripes

(**c**) 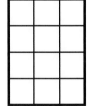 12 panes

2 For each tablecloth write the fraction coloured blue.

(**a**)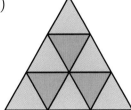

(**b**)

(**c**)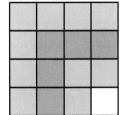

3 A group of footballers are at a training session. What fraction of the group is:

(**a**) wearing a woolly hat

(**b**) wearing shorts

(**c**) wearing goalkeeper's gloves

(**d**) dressed in a tracksuit?

4 Write these fractions in order, starting with the smallest.

$$\frac{1}{4}, \quad \frac{1}{2}, \quad \frac{1}{10}, \quad \frac{1}{3}, \quad \frac{1}{8}$$

5 Calculate:

(**a**) $\frac{1}{2}$ of £48   (**b**) $\frac{1}{2}$ of 32 kg   (**c**) $\frac{1}{2}$ of £5   (**d**) $\frac{1}{2}$ of 500 ml

6 Calculate:

(**a**) $\frac{1}{4}$ of £36   (**b**) $\frac{1}{8}$ of 48 tonnes   (**c**) $\frac{1}{10}$ of 30 g   (**d**) $\frac{1}{7}$ of 49 litres

7 In the special Halloween Bumper Pack there are 36 lollipops.
$\frac{1}{4}$ are orange, $\frac{1}{3}$ are lemon, $\frac{1}{6}$ are raspberry and the rest are blackcurrant.

How many lollipops are:

(**a**) orange   (**b**) lemon   (**c**) raspberry   (**d**) blackcurrant?

Summary

Understanding fractions

The pole has 5 equal stripes.

3 of the stripes are green.

$\frac{3}{5}$ of the pole is green.

$\frac{2}{5}$ of the pole is white.

The bigger the number on the bottom … the smaller the fraction.

$\frac{1}{2}$ is bigger than $\frac{1}{5}$

   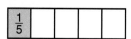

Calculating a fraction of a quantity

To find $\frac{1}{4}$, divide by 4
$\frac{1}{4}$ of £12 = £12 ÷ 4
         = **£3**

To find $\frac{1}{8}$, divide by 8
$\frac{1}{8}$ of 56 g = 56 g ÷ 8
         = **7 g**

To find $\frac{1}{10}$, divide by 10
$\frac{1}{10}$ of 250 kg   = 250 kg ÷ 10
         = **25 kg**

4 Angles

In this chapter you will learn to work with angles.

4.1 Turning

An **angle** is an amount of **turn**.

Cal is facing Nick.

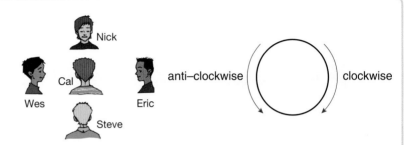

If he makes a half turn he will be facing Steve.

If he makes a quarter turn **clockwise** he will be facing Eric.

If he makes a quarter turn **anti-clockwise** he will be facing Wes.

If Cal makes a complete turn he will still be facing Nick.

A **quarter turn** is also called a **right angle**.

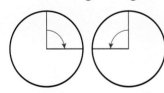

A **half turn** is the same as 2 right angles.

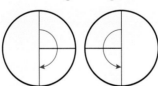

A **complete turn** is the same as 4 right angles.

Exercise 4.1

1 John is standing in the middle of the football pitch shown.
He is facing the North stand.
Which stand will he be facing if he makes a:

(**a**) half turn

(**b**) quarter turn clockwise

(**c**) full turn?

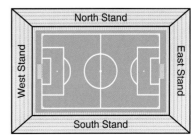

W You need Worksheets **4.1**, **4.2** and **4.3** for questions **2** to **6**.

7 Write the direction and angle needed to turn the dial from the position in diagram 1 to the position in the other diagrams.

Diagram 1

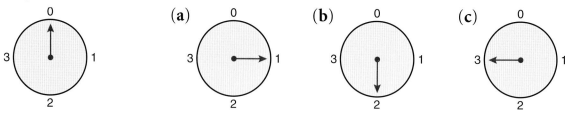

4.2 Naming angles

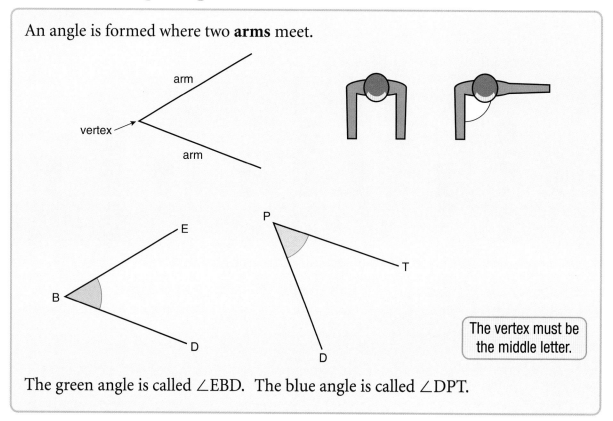

An angle is formed where two **arms** meet.

The green angle is called ∠EBD. The blue angle is called ∠DPT.

The vertex must be the middle letter.

Exercise 4.2

1 Name each marked angle.

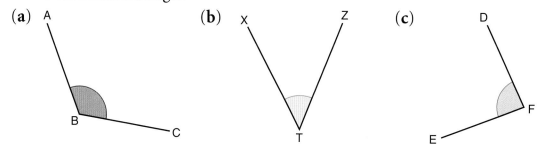

(d) 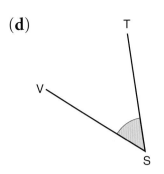 **(e)** 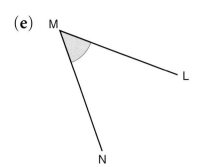 **(f)**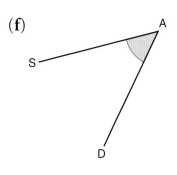

2 ABCD is a square. EFGH is a rectangle.
For each diagram name the angle which is:
(i) red   **(ii)** blue   **(iii)** yellow   **(iv)** green.

(a) 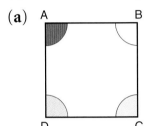 **(b)**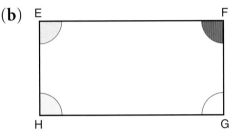

3 Sketch this triangle. Mark each angle in the colour given.
   (a) blue ∠ABC   **(b)** red ∠BAC   **(c)** green ∠ACB

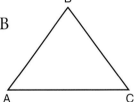

4.3 Types of angles

Remember
One right angle is a $\frac{1}{4}$ turn.

Two right angles joined together make a **straight angle**.

Exercise 4.3

1 You need a scrap of paper.
   (a) Fold the paper in half.
      You have formed a straight angle.
   (b) Now fold it again.
      You have now formed a right angle.
   (c) Use your right angle to check that the corners of your jotter are right angled.

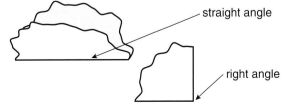

W You need Worksheet **4.4** for question **2**.

3 Make a list of ten objects in the classroom which contain a right angle.

4 Look at the clocks.

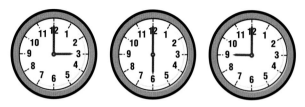

Write down the times when the hands form:
(**a**) a right angle   (**b**) a straight angle.

5 Name the two straight angles in each diagram.
(Use 3 letters for each angle.)

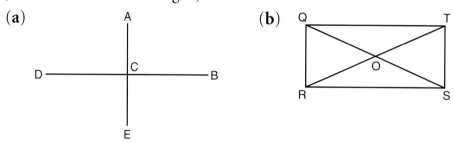

(**a**)

(**b**)

6 Make a list of five objects in the classroom which contain a straight angle.

4.4 More types of angle

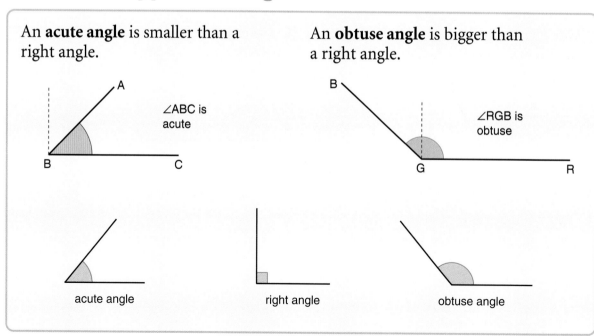

An **acute angle** is smaller than a right angle.

An **obtuse angle** is bigger than a right angle.

∠ABC is acute

∠RGB is obtuse

acute angle   right angle   obtuse angle

Exercise 4.4

1 List the angles that are:
(**a**) acute
(**b**) obtuse.

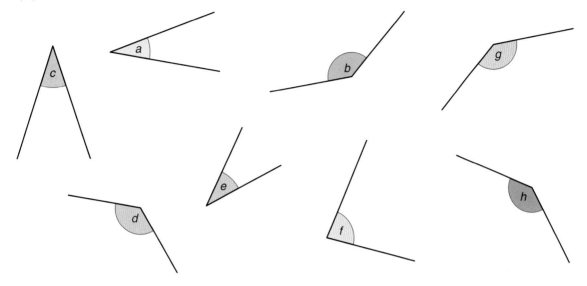

2 Look at the diagram. Write the colour of:
(**a**) a right angle
(**b**) a straight angle
(**c**) an acute angle
(**d**) an obtuse angle.

3 Name each angle and state whether it is acute or obtuse.

(**a**)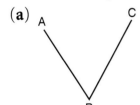

(**b**)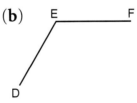

(**c**)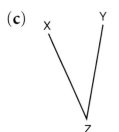

(**d**)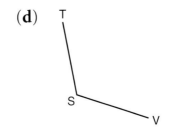

4.5 Measuring angles

Step 1 Place the centre of the protractor on the angle as shown.

Step 2 Use the scale which has a zero on an arm of the angle. Count round and read the value where the other arm passes through the scale.

Step 3 Write the size of the angle.

The angle is 40°.

Exercise 4.5

1 Write the size of the angle in each diagram.

(a)

(b)

(c)

(d)

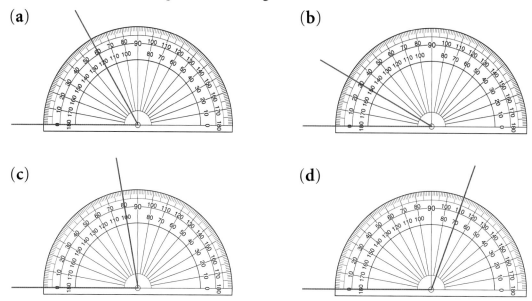

2 Measure the size of each angle.

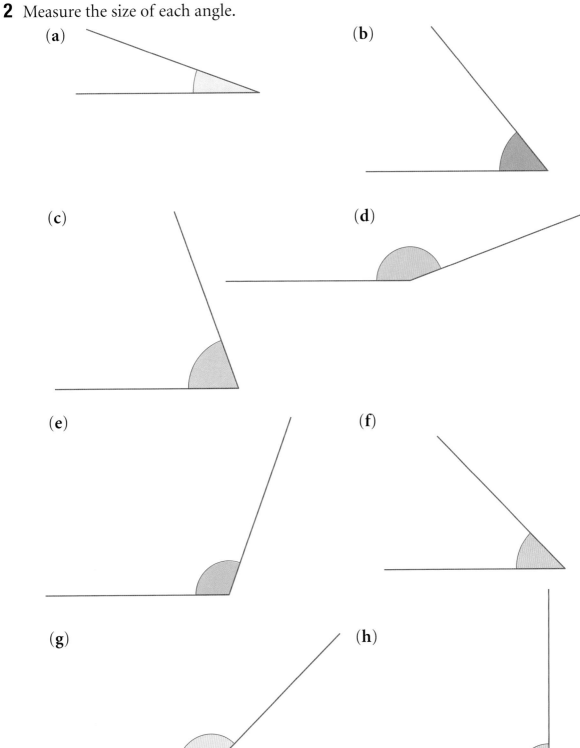

(a)

(b)

(c)

(d)

(e)

(f)

(g)

(h)

3 The last angle you measured was a right angle.
  (a) How many degrees are in a right angle?
  (b) How many degrees are in a straight angle?

4.6 Drawing angles

You need a ruler and a protractor to draw angles

Example
Draw ∠ABC = 30°

A ————————————————————— B

Step 1 Draw line AB 6 cm long.

Step 2 Place the centre of the protractor on B
with the base line on AB as shown.

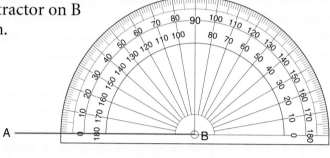

Step 3 Find the zero which
is on the line AB.
Count up to 30° and put a dot.

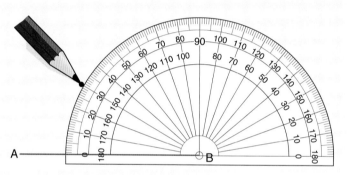

Step 4 Draw a line from B through the dot and mark C.

Step 5 Label your angle as shown.

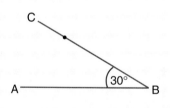

Exercise 4.6

W You need Worksheet **4.5** for question **1**.

2 Draw accurately the following angles.
   (**a**) ∠ABC = 50°   (**b**) ∠ABC = 20°   (**c**) ∠ABC = 40°   (**d**) ∠ABC = 80°

3 Draw accurately the following angles.
   (**a**) ∠XYZ = 60°   (**b**) ∠DEF = 10°   (**c**) ∠GHI = 65°   (**d**) ∠JKL = 90°
   (**e**) ∠MNO = 25°   (**f**) ∠PQR = 45°   (**g**) ∠STU = 75°   (**h**) ∠VWX = 110°
   (**i**) ∠SFA = 140°   (**j**) ∠DAT = 135°   (**k**) ∠ANG = 165°   (**l**) ∠KOP = 180°

4.7 Giving directions

Look at the map. This set of directions shows how Umar walks from A to B.

Start at A.
Walk 1 block North.
Turn right 90°.
Walk 2 blocks.
Turn left 90°.
Walk 1 block.
Turn left 90°.
Walk 2 blocks.

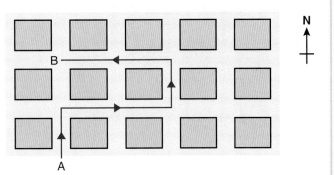

Exercise 4.7

You need Worksheet **4.6** for question **1**. You need red, green and blue pencils.

2 (**a**) The red line shows the route for Bob's paper round. Write down a set of directions for this route.

(**b**) The blue line shows the route for Rachael's paper round. Write down a set of directions for this route.

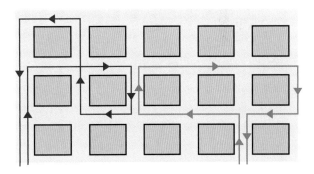

Review exercise 4

You need a protractor for questions **5** and **6**.

1 John is standing in the middle of the football pitch. He is facing the North stand.
Which stand will he be facing if he makes a

(**a**) half turn

(**b**) quarter turn clockwise

(**c**) full turn?

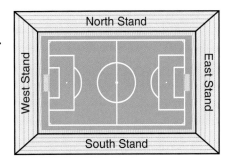

2 Name each angle.

(**a**) 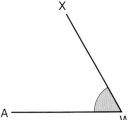   (**b**) 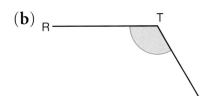   (**c**)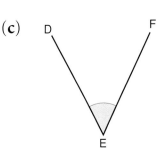

3 Sketch the door. Mark all the right angles.

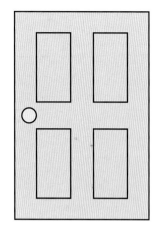

4 Copy each diagram. Write the type of angle for each.

   (**a**) 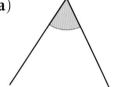   (**b**)    (**c**)   (**d**)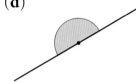

5 Measure the size of each angle, using a protractor.

   (**a**) 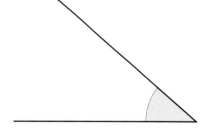   (**b**)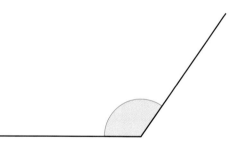

6 Draw accurately the following angles, using a protractor.
   (**a**) $\angle ABC = 60°$ (**b**) $\angle KLM = 130°$
   (**c**) $\angle XYZ = 35°$ (**a**) $\angle STV = 155°$

7 The green line shows the route P.C. Anderson walks.
   Write a set of directions for this route.

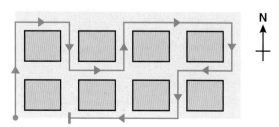

Summary

Turning

A quarter turn is called
a **right angle**.

A **half turn** is
2 right angles.

A **complete turn** is
4 right angles.

Naming angles

An angle is formed where two **arms** meet.

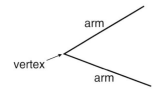

The angle is called ∠ABC.

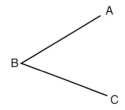

Types of angles

A **right angle**
is 90°.

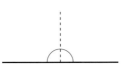

A **straight angle**
is 180°.

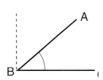

An **acute angle**
is smaller than
a right angle.

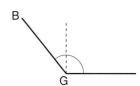

An **obtuse angle**
is bigger than a
right angle.

Measuring angles

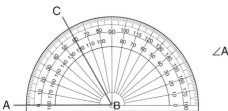

∠ABC = 60°

Drawing angles

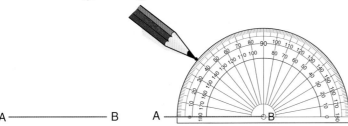

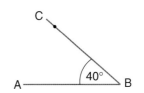

5 Decimals

In this chapter you will review decimal calculations.

5.1 Using money

Money may be expressed in pence (**p**) or in pounds (**£**).

Example 1
Write each amount in pounds (£):

£1 = 100 p

(a) → **£2.15**   (b) → **£0.08**

Example 2
Write in pence (p):

(a) → **300 p**   (b) → **210 p**

The decimal point separates the pounds and pence.

£8.62

pounds   ten pences   pence

Exercise 5.1

W You need Worksheet **5.1** for questions **1**, **2** and **3**.

4 Change each amount to pounds:

325 p = £3.25

(a) 325 p   (b) 619 p   (c) 903 p   (d) 78 p

(e) 530 p   (f) 98 p   (g) 20 p   (h) 6 p

(i) 50 p   (j) 2 p   (k) 1410 p   (l) 1020 p

5 Change each amount to pence:

£7.23 = 723 p

(a) £7.23   (b) £9.25   (c) £4.80   (d) £1.06

(e) £0.75   (f) £0.80   (g) £0.09   (h) £10.02

5.2 Adding money

When adding money, the decimal points must be in line.

Example 1

```
   £3.62
+  £2.09
  ─────
   £5.71
     ↑
```

Example 2

Find £12.56 + £3.67.

```
   £12.56
+   £3.67
  ──────
   £16.23
      ↑
```

Exercise 5.2

V You need Worksheet **5.2** for questions **1**, **2** and **3**.

4 Copy and complete:

(**a**)
```
   £15.08
+   £5.35
  ──────

```

(**b**)
```
   £14.81
+   £5.29
  ──────

```

(**c**)
```
   £19.91
+  £11.99
  ──────

```

5 Find:

(**a**) £4.50 + £3.47   (**b**) £0.75 + £1.18   (**c**) £6.42 + £2.28

(**d**) £7.90 + £0.09   (**e**) £9.99 + £4.02   (**f**) £8.41 + 932p

6 Find the total amount for each pair of bags:

(**a**) 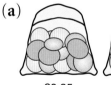   (**b**) 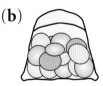   (**c**)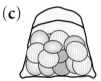

£8.35   £1.75   £6.57   £3.77   £9.09   £19.92

7 Copy and complete each bill:

(**a**)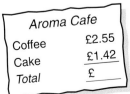

Aroma Cafe
Coffee	£2.55
Cake	£1.42
Total	£

(**b**)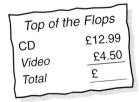

Top of the Flops
CD	£12.99
Video	£4.50
Total	£

(**c**)

Bill's Garage
Parts	£12.99
Labour	£29.55
Total	£

V You need Worksheet **5.3** for questions **8**, **9** and **10**.

5.3 Subtracting money

When subtracting money, the decimal points must be in line.

Example 1

$$\begin{array}{r} £3.69 \\ - \ £2.04 \\ \hline \textbf{£1.65} \\ \hline \end{array}$$

Example 2

Find £4.86 − £2.67.

$$\begin{array}{r} £4.\overset{7}{\cancel{8}}\overset{1}{6} \\ - \ £2.67 \\ \hline \textbf{£2.19} \\ \hline \end{array}$$

Exercise 5.3

W You need Worksheet **5.4** for questions **1**, **2** and **3**.

4 Copy and complete:

(**a**)
$$\begin{array}{r} £12.09 \\ - \ £1.22 \\ \hline \end{array}$$

(**b**)
$$\begin{array}{r} £12.31 \\ - \ £6.29 \\ \hline \end{array}$$

(**c**)
$$\begin{array}{r} £18.98 \\ - \ £9.99 \\ \hline \end{array}$$

5 Find:

(**a**) £3.67 − £1.23   (**b**) £6.75 − £2.31   (**c**) £9.97 − £7.57

(**d**) £8.42 − £5.18   (**e**) £5.62 − £3.75   (**f**) £5 − £1.79

(**g**) £6.03 − £0.07   (**h**) £10.09 − £5.18   (**i**) £16.37 − 1059 p

W You need Worksheet **5.5** for questions **6**, **7**, **8** and **9**.

10 (**a**) Bill has £8.35 change from a £20 note.
How much did he spend?

(**b**) Sara has £7.81 change from **three** £10 notes.
How much did she spend?

11 Jo buys a doll for £4.95 and a pram for £7.66.
She gives the shopkeeper four five pound notes.
The shopkeeper gives her £3.75 change.
How much is missing from her change?

5.4 Using a calculator

In money calculations there must be two numbers after the decimal point.

Example 1

What would these amounts look like on a calculator?

£2.54 → ┌──────────┐
         │   2.54 │
         └──────────┘

£1.02 → ┌──────────┐
         │   1.02 │
         └──────────┘

Example 2

Write in pounds the amounts shown on each calculator:

┌──────────┐
│   0.24 │ → £0.24
└──────────┘

┌──────────┐
│   0.6   │ → £0.60
└──────────┘

> Two numbers after the decimal point

Example 3

Find £3.35 × 2

[3] [.] [3] [5] [×] [2] [=]   ┌──────────┐
                                │   6.7   │
                                └──────────┘

Answer is **£6.70**.

Exercise 5.4

You need Worksheet **5.6** for questions **1**, **2**, **3** and **4**.

5 Find:

(a) £2.35 + £1.82 + £7.90
(b) £1.80 + £5.79 + £8.45
(c) £14.99 + £2.50 + £2.41
(d) £3.03 + £1.76 + £8.01
(e) £32.10 + £64
(f) £33 + £11.90 + £22
(g) £37.37 + £21.23
(h) £16 + £1.52 + 35 p

> 35 p = £0.35

6 Find:

(a) £6.84 − £2.63   (b) £5.67 − £2.29   (c) £8.21 − £6.96
(d) £4.07 − £3.68   (e) £5.70 − £3   (f) £7 − £4.70

7 Calculate:

(a) £4.45 × 2   (b) £1.66 × 5   (c) £2.75 × 4   (d) £6.44 × 5
(e) £0.06 × 5   (f) £1.45 × 10   (g) £1.20 × 100 (h) £6.25 × 20

8 Calculate:

(a) £5.45 ÷ 5   (b) £2.40 ÷ 2   (c) £3.60 ÷ 4   (d) £12.30 ÷ 3
(e) £1.60 ÷ 2   (f) £4.90 ÷ 7   (g) £32.64 ÷ 8   (h) £8 ÷ 10

9 Jake has £2.40, Mil has £1.75 and Bella has £2.
How much do they have altogether?

10 Isha has £8.
She buys a scarf.
How much does she have left?

11 Bobby gets £3.50 from his uncle, £2.80 from
his aunt and £6.70 from his grandad.
How much does Bobby get in total?

12 Brad has a £10 note.
He buys a magazine and a box of sweets.
How much does Brad have left?

13 Paul has a £5 note.
He buys sweets at £2.65, juice at 55p and
a comic at £1.40.
Does Paul have enough to buy crisps at 35p?

14 Baz has five bags of money.
There is £3.40 in each bag.
How much has Baz altogether?

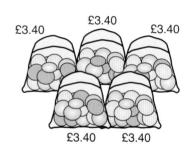

15 Jon has to share £5.60 equally among
eight people.
How much will each person get?

16 Bob has four pockets.
He has £0.60 in each pocket.
How much has Bob in total?

17 Five people share equally a prize of £12.
How much will each person receive?

18 Mary has three bags, each with £4.40.
Bill has two bags, each with £6.45.
Taz has a piggy bank with £5 in it.
How much do they have altogether?

Review exercise 5

1 Write each amount in pounds:

(**a**) 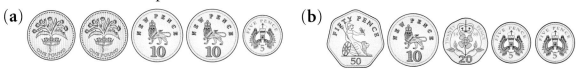   (**b**)

2 Write each amount in pounds:

(**a**) 356 p   (**b**) 860 p   (**c**) 67 p   (**d**) 2 p

3 Write in pence:

(**a**) £5.75   (**b**) £1.80   (**c**) £3.05   (**d**) £0.10

4 Copy and complete:

(**a**)   £1.45   (**b**)   £2.51   (**c**)   £2.62
       + £2.34   + £1.29   + £3.69
       _____   _____   _____

(**d**)   £3.25   (**e**)   £6.36   (**f**)   £0.92
              2.35   £3.43   £9.61
       + £1.45   + £0.12   + £8.69
       _____   _____   _____

(**g**)   £3.36   (**h**)   £5.51   (**i**)   £2.42
       − £1.12   − £2.37   − £1.69
       _____   _____   _____

5 Find:

(**a**) £4.65 + £1.31   (**b**) £6.46 − £2.87
(**c**) £5.61 − £4.93   (**d**) £1.12 + £2.33 + £2.51
(**e**) £2.65 + £3.14 + £1.14   (**f**) £3.66 + £4.78 + £5.67

6 Jack has £5.
He buys a comic and sweets.
How much change will Jack be given?

7 Write in pounds the amount shown on each calculator:

(**a**)   (**b**)   (**c**)

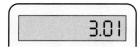 

8 Use a calculator to find:

(a) £1.24 × 5   (b) £4.80 ÷ 6   (c) £2.80 ÷ 7

9 Five people share equally a bill of £18.
How much will each pay?

Summary

Using money

Money may be expressed in pence (**p**) or in pounds (**£**).

        may be written as 215 p or £2.15

Addition/subtraction

When adding or subtracting money, the decimal points must be in line.

$$
\begin{array}{r}
£2.52 \\
+\ £1.09 \\
\hline
£3.61 \\
\uparrow
\end{array}
\qquad
\begin{array}{r}
£\overset{1}{1}\overset{1}{2}.\overset{14}{5}\overset{1}{6} \\
-\ £3.67 \\
\hline
£8.89 \\
\uparrow
\end{array}
$$

Using a calculator

In money calculations there must be two numbers after the decimal point.

£4.65 ⟶ | 4.65 |

£0.23 ⟶ | 0.23 |

£0.20 ⟶ | 0.2 |

6 Measurement

In this chapter you will revise how to measure using the metric system.

6.1 Length

You may use common objects to estimate measurements before measuring accurately.

The height of a door is about 2 metres.

The thickness of this book is about 1 centimetre.

Exercise 6.1

You need Worksheet **6.1** for questions **1**, **2** and **3**. You need scissors and glue.

4 Estimate the length of each of these lines in centimetres.

(**a**) —————

(**b**) ————————————

(**c**) ——————————————————

(**d**) —————————

5 (**a**) Which of these lines do you think is the longer?

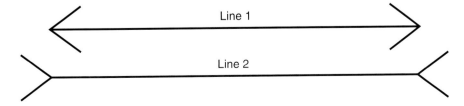

Line 1

Line 2

(**b**) Trace Line 1 and check its size against Line 2.

6 Estimate the following sizes in your classroom:
   (**a**) The width of your desk.
   (**b**) The height of the room.
   (**c**) The height of a window.
   (**d**) The length of the room.
   (**e**) The length of your pencil.
   (**f**) The width of this textbook.

6.2 Measuring

Sometimes you need to have accurate measurements.
How long is the caterpillar?

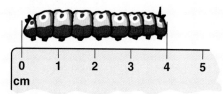

                                   The caterpillar is **4** centimetres long.

Exercise 6.2

1 Write down the length of each caterpillar.

  (**a**)   (**b**)   (**c**)

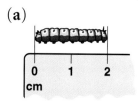   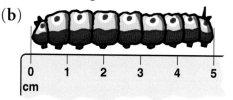 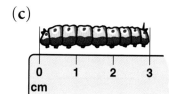

  (**d**)

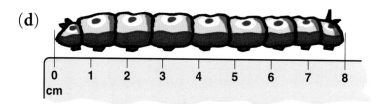

  (**e**)

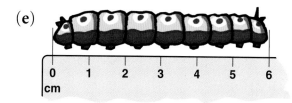

2 Draw horizontal lines of length:

(**a**) 6 cm   (**b**) 8 cm   (**c**) 10 cm   (**d**) 9 cm   (**e**) 15 cm

3 Use a ruler to measure the lengths of these model cars.

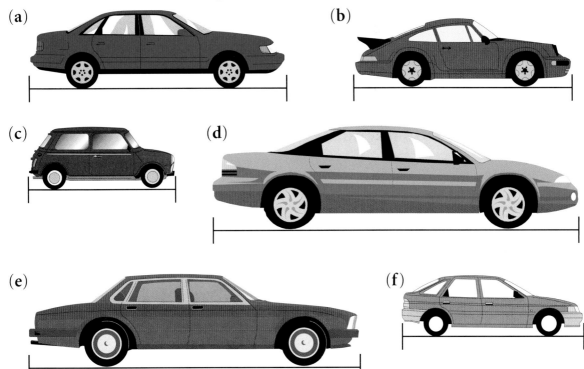

(**a**)   (**b**)

(**c**)   (**d**)

(**e**)   (**f**)

4 Measure this hand span:

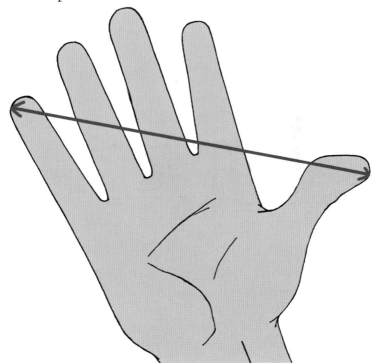

5 (**a**) Stretch your own hand as wide as you can.

(**b**) Draw around it in your jotter.

(**c**) Measure your hand span.

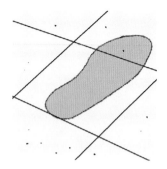

6 You need a sheet of A4 paper.

(**a**) Draw around your shoe on the paper.

(**b**) Measure the length of your drawing.

7 (**a**) Estimate the width of this book.

(**b**) Measure the width of the book.

(**c**) Compare your estimate with the true width.

8 Repeat question 7 for the height of this page.

9 You need a measuring tape or metre stick.

(**a**) Estimate the width of your classroom.

(**b**) Measure the width of the classroom.

(**c**) Compare your estimate with the true width.

10 Repeat question **9** for the length of your classroom.

11 Work with a partner. You need a measuring tape or metre stick.

(**a**) Estimate the length and width of the nearest football pitch.

(**b**) Measure the length and width of the pitch.

(**c**) Compare your estimate with the true lengths.

6.3 Metres and centimetres

Remember 100 centimetres = 1 metre

Example 1

Change the following into metres or metres and centimetres.

(**a**) 200 centimetres

200 cm = **2 m**

(**b**) 125 centimetres

125 cm = **1 m 25 cm**

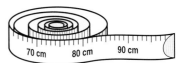

Example 2

Change the following into centimetres.

(**a**) 5 metres

5 m = **500 cm**

(**b**) 4 metres 55 centimetres

4 m 55 cm = 400 cm + 55 cm = **455 cm**

Exercise 6.3

1 Write each of the following in metres and centimetres:

(**a**) 300 cm   (**b**) 600 cm   (**c**) 500 cm   (**d**) 900 cm

(**e**) 1100 cm   (**f**) 1900 cm   (**g**) 2000 cm   (**h**) 2500 cm

(**i**) 325 cm   (**j**) 485 cm   (**k**) 550 cm   (**l**) 50 cm

2 Write each of the following in centimetres:

(**a**) 4 m   (**b**) 7 m   (**c**) 8 m   (**d**) 12 m

(**e**) 8 m 50 cm   (**f**) 6 m 25 cm   (**g**) 2 m 75 cm   (**h**) 3 m 15 cm

(**i**) 25 m   (**j**) 33 m   (**k**) 42 m   (**l**) 55 m

3 Work with a partner. You need a measuring tape or metre stick.

(**a**) Estimate your height in metres and centimetres.

(**b**) Measure your height.

(**c**) Compare your estimate with your true height.

My height is 5'3" or 1 metre 60 centimetres.

4 Repeat question 3 for your partner's height.

5 Work with a partner. You need a measuring tape.
For each person, measure the length of 5 paces.
Give your answers in metres and centimetres.

6 (**a**) Write the names of these people in order of height, shortest first.
(**b**) Write their heights in order starting with the tallest.

7 (**a**) Put these cars in order starting with the widest.

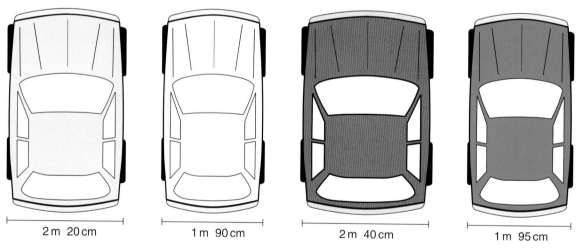

(**b**) Write the widths in order starting with the widest.

8 Arrange each of the following in order, smallest first:
(**a**) 5 m, 2 m, 8 m, 7 m
(**b**) 25 cm, 18 cm, 3 cm, 75 cm
(**c**) 5 m 25 cm, 5 m 19 cm, 6 m 2 cm, 3 m 99 cm
(**d**) 2 m 95 cm, 3 m 9 cm, 8 m 1 cm, 1 m 99 cm

6.4 Weight

Metric weight

You may use common objects to estimate weights before weighing accurately.
The weight of a pen is about 5 grammes.
The weight of a bag of sugar is 1 kilogramme.

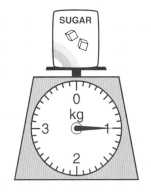

Remember
1000 grammes (g) = 1 kilogramme (kg)

Example 1
Change the following into kilogrammes or kilogrammes and grammes.

(**a**) 3000 grammes

3000 g = **3 kg**

(**b**) 2500 grammes

2500 g = 2000 + 500 g = **2 kg 500 g**

Example 2
Change the following into grammes.

(**a**) 5 kilogrammes

5 kg = **5000 g**

(**b**) 3 kilogrammes 500 grammes

3 kg 500 g = 3000 g + 500 g = **3500 g**

Exercise 6.4

1 Put these birds in order of weight. Start with the lightest.

Golden Eagle

Parrot

Magpie

Swan

Hummingbird

2 Read the weights on each of these bathroom scales.

(a)

(b)

(c)

(d)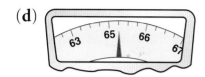

(e)

(f)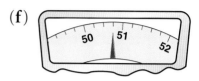

3 Work with a partner. You need bathroom scales.
   (a) Estimate your weight in kilogrammes.
   (b) Measure your weight.
   (c) Estimate your partner's weight.
   (d) Measure your partner's weight.
   (e) Check your estimates against the real weights.

4 Write the following in kilogrammes and grammes:
   (a) 4000 g   (b) 6000 g   (c) 9000 g   (d) 7000 g
   (e) 4500 g   (f) 7500 g   (g) 5500 g   (h) 1500 g
   (i) 2300 g   (j) 3600 g   (k) 8900 g   (l) 4200 g

5 Write each of the following in grammes:
   (a) 4 kg   (b) 6 kg   (c) 9 kg   (d) 7 kg
   (e) 5 kg 500 g   (f) 3 kg 400 g   (g) 8 kg 200 g   (h) 4 kg 200 g
   (i) 2 kg 700 g   (j) 6 kg 900 g   (k) 7 kg 300 g   (l) 8 kg 700 g

6.5 Volume

Metric volume

The volume of liquid in a container may be measured in litres.

This carton contains 1 litre.

This bottle of cola contains 2 litres.

This bottle contains $\frac{1}{2}$ litre.

Exercise 6.5

1 Write the volume of liquid in each jug in litres.

(**a**)

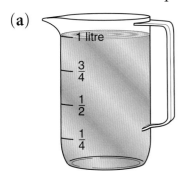

(**b**)

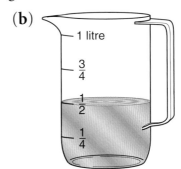

(**c**)

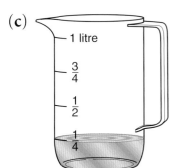

(**d**)

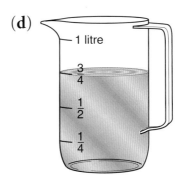

2 You need an empty 1 litre juice bottle and an empty 500 millilitre bottle.
(**a**) Fill the 500 millilitre bottle with water.
(**b**) Pour this into the large bottle.
(**c**) Repeat this until the large bottle is full.
(**d**) How many times did you pour the small into the larger one?
(**e**) Copy and complete this sentence.
500 millilitres = ☐ litre.

3 You need an empty 1 litre juice bottle and an empty 250 millilitre bottle.
(**a**) Fill the 250 millilitre bottle with water.
(**b**) Pour this into the large bottle.
(**c**) Repeat this until the large bottle is full.
(**d**) How many times did you pour the small into the larger one?
(**e**) Copy and complete this sentence.
250 millilitres = ☐ litre.

4 How many millilitres are there in a litre?

Review exercise 6

1 Write down the length of each screw.
(**a**)
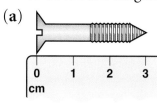
(**b**)
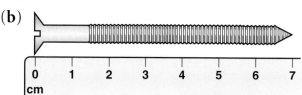

2 Draw horizontal lines of length:
(**a**) 5 cm   (**b**) 7 cm   (**c**) 12 cm

3 Write each of the following in metres and centimetres:
(**a**) 400 cm   (**b**) 800 cm   (**c**) 450 cm   (**d**) 620 cm

4 Write each of the following in centimetres:
(**a**) 5 m   (**b**) 9 m   (**c**) 2 m 50 cm   (**d**) 3 m 25 cm

5 Arrange each set in order, starting with the smallest.
(**a**) 6 m,   3 m,   4 m,   9 m
(**b**) 25 cm,   23 cm,   26 cm,   22 cm
(**c**) 3 m 15 cm,   3 m 8 cm,   7 m 15 cm,   99 cm

6 Write the following in kilogrammes and grammes:

(**a**) 5000 g   (**b**) 8000 g   (**c**) 6500 g   (**d**) 8200 g

7 Write each of the following in grammes:

(**a**) 2 kg   (**b**) 3 kg   (**c**) 7 kg 500 g   (**d**) 9 kg 300 g

8 Write the volume of liquid in each jug in litres.

(**a**)

(**b**)

Summary

Length

100 centimetres (cm) = 1 metre (m)

Weight

1000 gramme (g) = 1 kilogramme (kg)

Volume

1000 millilitres = 1 litre

7 Perimeter and area

In this chapter you will learn about perimeters and areas of simple shapes.

7.1 Perimeter

The **perimeter** of a shape is the **total distance** around the outside edge. The units millimetre, centimetre, metre and kilometre are used to measure perimeters.

Example 1
Calculate the perimeter of the stamp.

21 mm

18 mm

$$\text{Perimeter} = \text{length} + \text{breadth} + \text{length} + \text{breadth}$$
$$= 21 + 18 + 21 + 18$$
$$= 78 \text{ mm}$$

Perimeter of stamp = 78 mm.

Example 2
Calculate the perimeter of the car sticker.

15 cm   12 cm
Skye
18 cm

$$\text{Perimeter} = \text{side} + \text{side} + \text{side}$$
$$= 18 + 15 + 12$$
$$= 45 \text{ cm}$$

Perimeter of sticker = 45 cm.

Exercise 7.1

1 Calculate the perimeter of each shape.

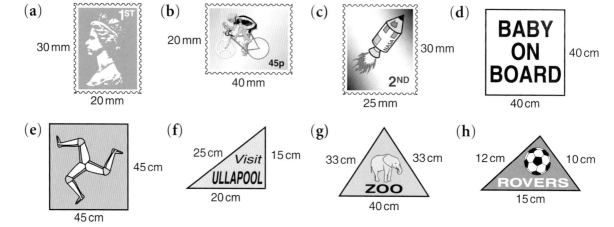

(a) 30 mm, 20 mm

(b) 20 mm, 40 mm

(c) 30 mm, 25 mm

(d) 40 cm, 40 cm — BABY ON BOARD

(e) 45 cm, 45 cm

(f) 25 cm, 15 cm, 20 cm — Visit ULLAPOOL

(g) 33 cm, 33 cm, 40 cm — ZOO

(h) 12 cm, 10 cm, 15 cm — ROVERS

2 Calculate the perimeter of each shape.

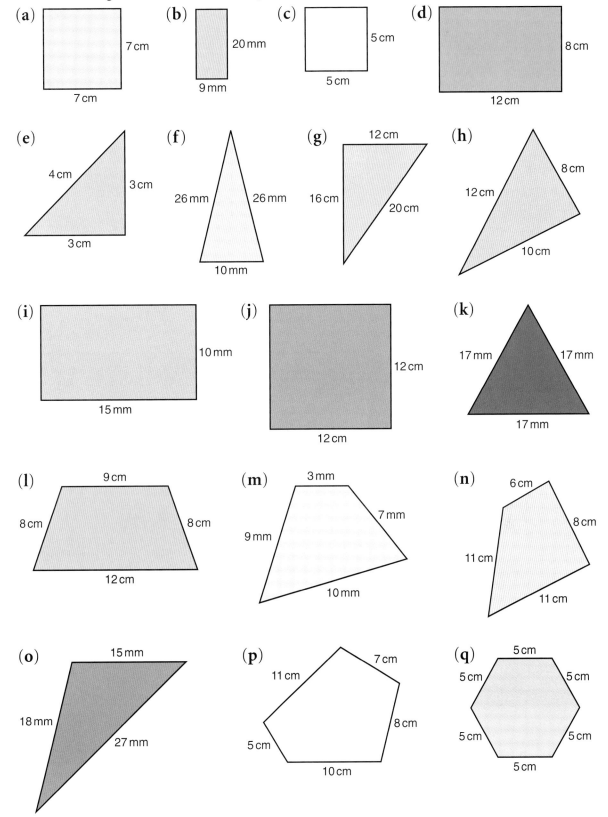

(a) 7 cm, 7 cm

(b) 20 mm, 9 mm

(c) 5 cm, 5 cm

(d) 8 cm, 12 cm

(e) 4 cm, 3 cm, 3 cm

(f) 26 mm, 26 mm, 10 mm

(g) 12 cm, 16 cm, 20 cm

(h) 8 cm, 12 cm, 10 cm

(i) 10 mm, 15 mm

(j) 12 cm, 12 cm

(k) 17 mm, 17 mm, 17 mm

(l) 9 cm, 8 cm, 8 cm, 12 cm

(m) 3 mm, 7 mm, 9 mm, 10 mm

(n) 6 cm, 8 cm, 11 cm, 11 cm

(o) 15 mm, 18 mm, 27 mm

(p) 7 cm, 11 cm, 8 cm, 5 cm, 10 cm

(q) 5 cm, 5 cm, 5 cm, 5 cm, 5 cm, 5 cm

W You need Worksheets **7.1** and **7.2** for questions **3**, **4** and **5**.

7.2 Area

The **area** of a shape is the amount of **surface** it covers.

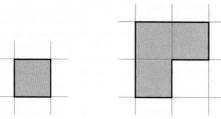 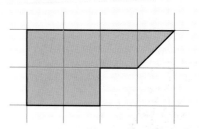

1 square centimetre   3 cm^2 $5\frac{1}{2}$ cm^2
is written as 1 cm^2.

Example

Find the area of this map.

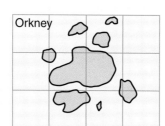

The map has 12 squares.

The area is 12 cm^2.

Exercise 7.2

1 These shapes are made from centimetre squares.
Find the area of each shape.

(a)
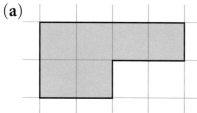

(b)
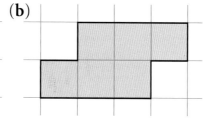

(c)
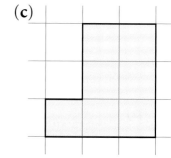

(d)
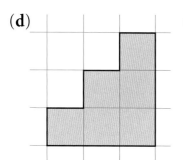

(e)
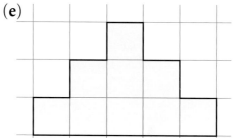

(f)
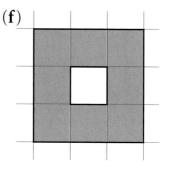

2 Find the area of each map.

(**a**)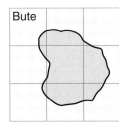

(**b**)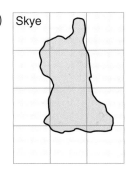

(**c**)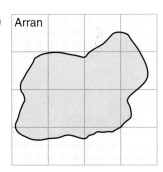

(**d**)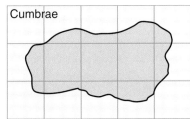

(**e**)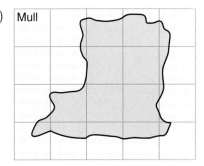

3 These shapes have been drawn on grids of centimetre squares.
Find the area of each shape.

(**a**)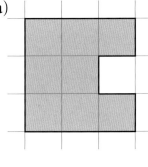

(**b**)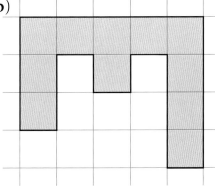

(**c**)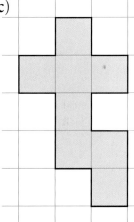

(**d**)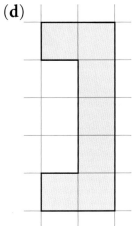

(**e**)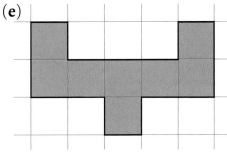

(**f**)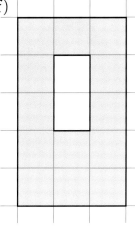

4 These shapes have been drawn on a grid of centimetre dots.
Find the area of each shape.

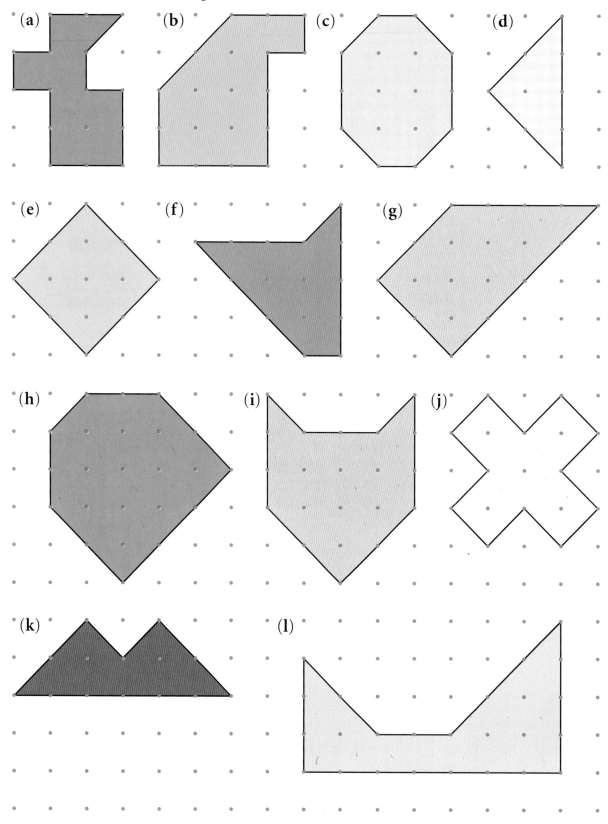

(a) (b) (c) (d)

(e) (f) (g)

(h) (i) (j)

(k) (l)

W You need Worksheet **7.3** and **7.4** for questions **5** and **6**.

7.3 A formula for the area of a rectangle

This rectangle has 3 rows.
Each row has 4 square centimetres.
The area of the rectangle = 3 × 4 = **12 cm²**.

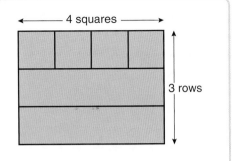

The area of a rectangle = length × breadth

Example
Calculate the area of this rectangle.

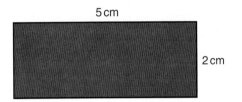

Area = 5 × 2 = 10
The area of the rectangle is 10 cm².

Exercise 7.3

1 Calculate the area of each rectangle.

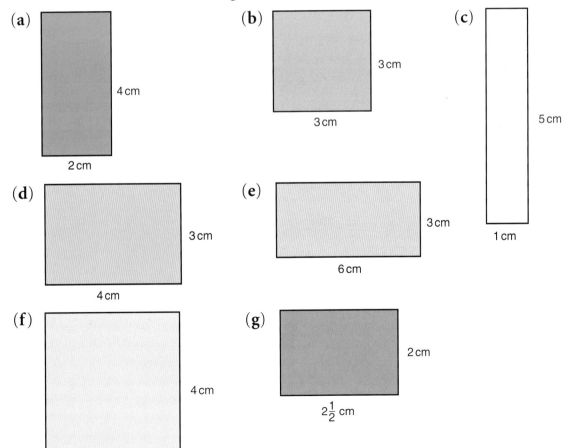

2 A photograph has length 11 cm and breadth 9 cm.
Calculate the area of the photograph.

3 The page of a notebook has length 15 cm and breadth 10 cm.
Calculate the area of the page.

4 Tiles in the kitchen are square and 10 cm along each side.
Calculate the area of a tile.

5 A postcard is 10 cm long and 6 cm wide.
Calculate the area of the postcard.

6 The page of a diary is 12 cm long and 8 cm wide.
Calculate the area of the page.

7 A square mosaic tile has sides of 9 cm.
Calculate the area of a tile.

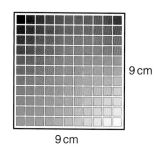

9 cm

9 cm

8 (**a**) Calculate the areas of these rectangles.

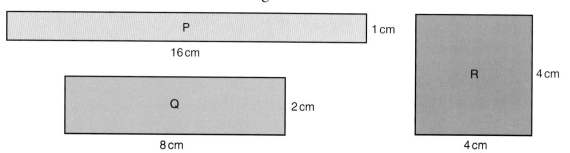

P
16 cm
1 cm

Q
8 cm
2 cm

R
4 cm
4 cm

(**b**) Calculate the areas of these rectangles.

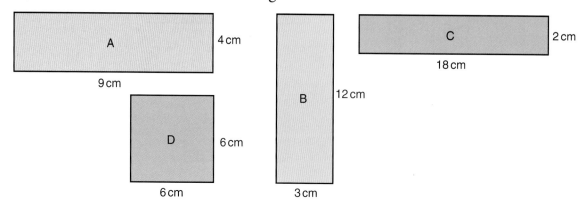

A
9 cm
4 cm

D
6 cm
6 cm

B
3 cm
12 cm

C
18 cm
2 cm

(**c**) Are all rectangles with the same area the same shape?

Review exercise 7

1 Calculate the perimeter of each shape.

(**a**)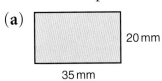
20 mm
35 mm

(**b**)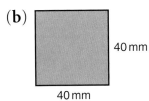
40 mm
40 mm

(**c**)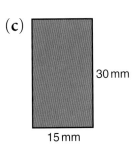
30 mm
15 mm

(**d**)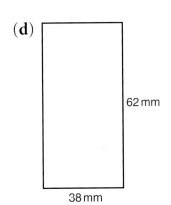
62 mm
38 mm

(**e**)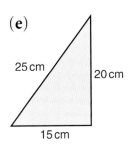
25 cm
20 cm
15 cm

(**f**)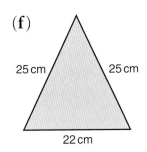
25 cm   25 cm
22 cm

(**g**)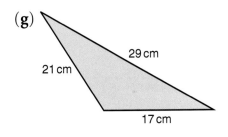
29 cm
21 cm
17 cm

(**h**)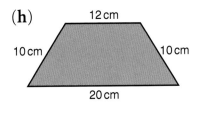
12 cm
10 cm   10 cm
20 cm

(**i**)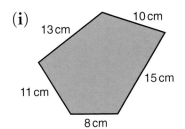
10 cm
13 cm
15 cm
11 cm
8 cm

(**j**)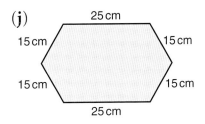
25 cm
15 cm   15 cm
15 cm   15 cm
25 cm

2 These shapes are made from centimetre squares. Find the area of each shape.

(**a**)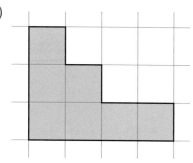

(**b**)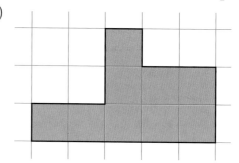

(**c**)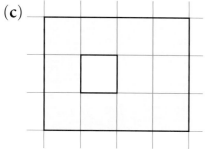

(**d**)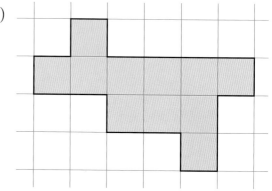

(**e**)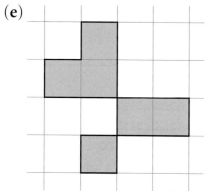

(**f**)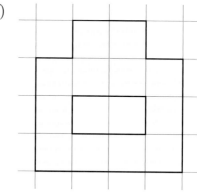

(**g**)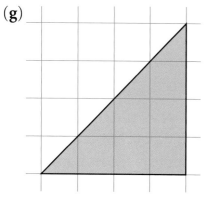

(**h**)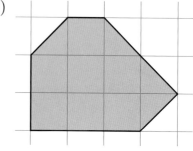

3 These shapes have been drawn on grids of centimetre squares.
Find the area of each shape.

(a)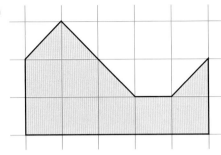

(b)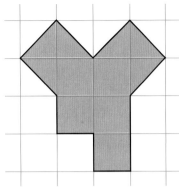

(c)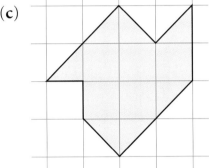

4 Calculate the area of each rectangle.

(a)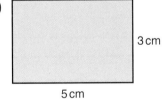
3 cm
5 cm

(b)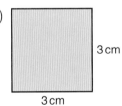
3 cm
3 cm

(c)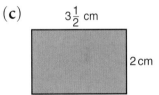
$3\frac{1}{2}$ cm
2 cm

5 A bathroom tile in Tiles-for-You has length 10 cm and breadth 15 cm.
Find the area of the tile.

6 The inside edges of a square photo frame are 8 cm.
Calculate the area of the photo which fits inside the frame.

Summary

Perimeter

The perimeter of a shape is the total distance round the edge.
Add the lengths of the sides to find the perimeter.

$$\text{Perimeter} = 3 + 5 + 2 + 2$$
$$= \mathbf{12\ cm}$$

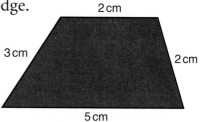

Area

The area of a shape is the amount of surface it covers.
Count the number of **square centimetres** to find area.

$$\text{Area} = \mathbf{6\ cm^2}$$

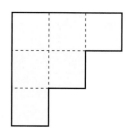

The area of a rectangle = length $\times$ breadth
$$= 4 \times 2$$
$$= \mathbf{8\ cm^2}$$

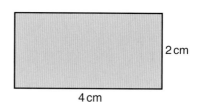

Different shapes can have the same area..

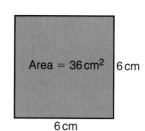

8 Time

In this chapter you will use 12 hour time in everyday situations.

8.1 Morning, afternoon, evening

7 o'clock in the morning

9 o'clock in the evening

Exercise 8.1

You need Worksheet **8.1** for questions **1** and **2**.

W **3** Use **morning**, **afternoon** and **evening** to say when you think each of these things happens.

(**a**) School starts.

(**b**) Newspapers are delivered.

(**c**) Eat breakfast.

(**d**) Street lights are turned on.

(**e**) Watch breakfast TV.

(**f**) School ends.

(**g**) Sun rises.

(**h**) Do homework.

(**i**) Sun sets.

(**j**) Go to bed.

8.2 Telling the time

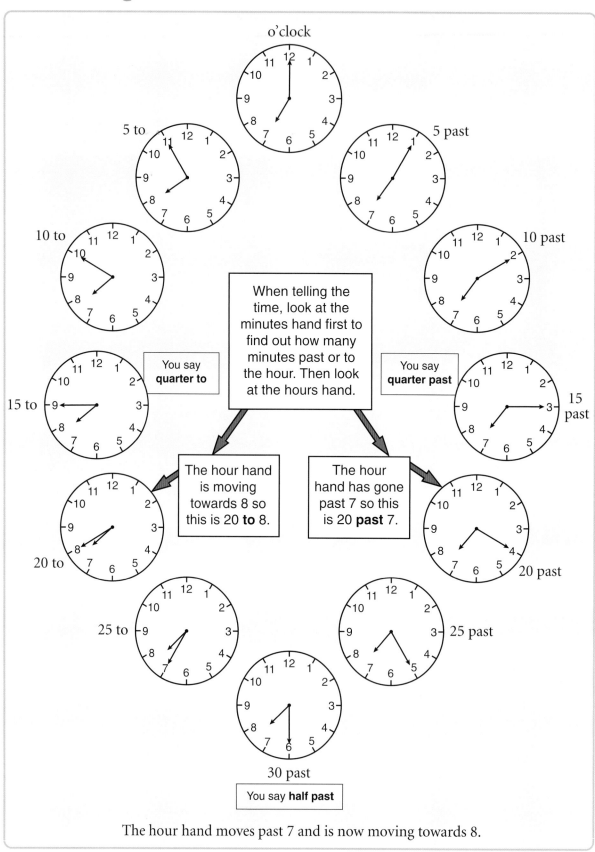

o'clock

5 to

5 past

10 to

10 past

When telling the time, look at the minutes hand first to find out how many minutes past or to the hour. Then look at the hours hand.

You say **quarter to**

You say **quarter past**

15 to

15 past

The hour hand is moving towards 8 so this is 20 **to** 8.

The hour hand has gone past 7 so this is 20 **past** 7.

20 to

20 past

25 to

25 past

30 past

You say **half past**

The hour hand moves past 7 and is now moving towards 8.

Exercise 8.2

You need Worksheets **8.2** and **8.3** for questions **1** and **2**.

3 Write the times shown on these clocks.

(**a**) 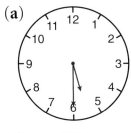   (**b**) 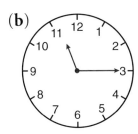   (**c**)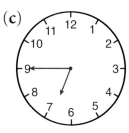

(**d**) 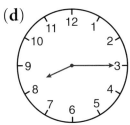   (**e**) 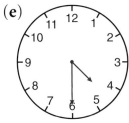   (**f**)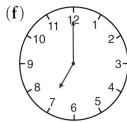

(**g**) 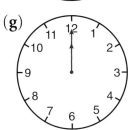   (**h**) 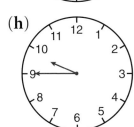   (**i**)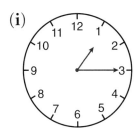

4 Write the times shown on these clocks.

(**a**) 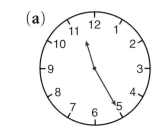   (**b**) 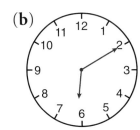   (**c**)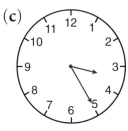

(**d**) 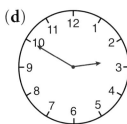   (**e**) 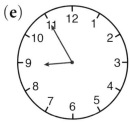   (**f**)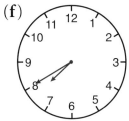

(**g**) 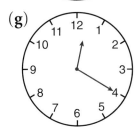   (**h**) 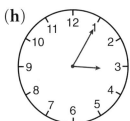   (**i**)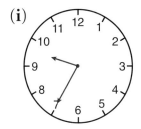

8.3 Digital clocks

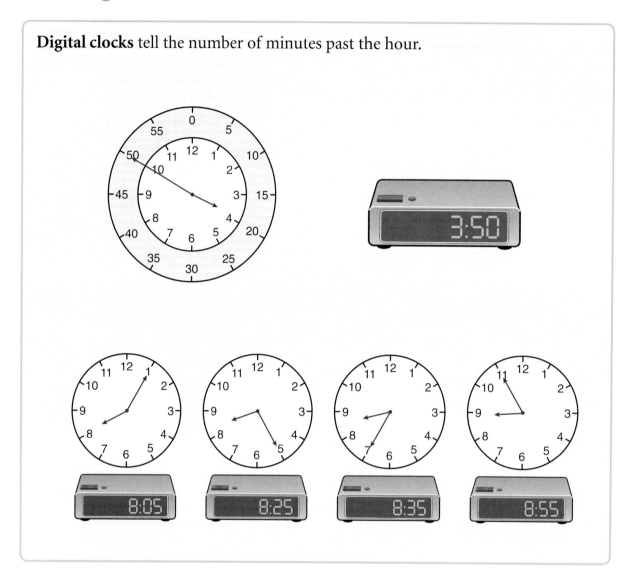

Digital clocks tell the number of minutes past the hour.

Exercise 8.3

W You need Worksheet **8.4** for question **1**.

2 Draw the display of a **digital** clock showing these times.

(**a**) twenty five past three   (**b**) quarter past ten

(**c**) five past eight   (**d**) ten to five

(**e**) half past eight   (**f**) twenty to seven

(**g**) twenty five to eleven   (**h**) quarter to six

`09:25`

W You need Worksheet **8.5** for question **3**.

4 Write these appointments into Mr Foster's diary on Worksheet **8.6** and complete the Worksheet:

Quarter to nine – assembly

Quarter to two – presentation

Quarter past two – meeting Mr & Mrs Jones

Nine o'clock – maths class (1 hour)

Quarter past eleven – interview B. Fogg

Half past eleven – meeting

Half past twelve – lunch

Quarter to three – playground duty

You need Worksheet **8.6** for question **5**.

8.4 a.m. and p.m.

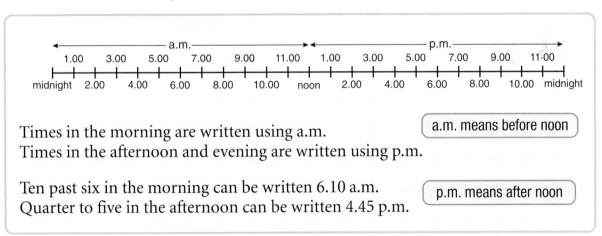

Times in the morning are written using a.m.
Times in the afternoon and evening are written using p.m.

> a.m. means before noon

Ten past six in the morning can be written 6.10 a.m.
Quarter to five in the afternoon can be written 4.45 p.m.

> p.m. means after noon

Exercise 8.4

1 Write the times for these events using a.m. or p.m.

(**a**) evening news   7.00

(**b**) lunch break   12.30

(**c**) go to school   8.00

(**d**) start paper round   7.30

(**e**) play football   4.30

(**f**) dentist's appointment   11.15

2 Write these times in figures using a.m. or p.m.

(**a**) quarter past six in the morning.

(**b**) half past three in the afternoon.

(**c**) twenty to seven in the evening.

(**d**) twenty five past twelve in the afternoon.

(**e**) ten to nine in the morning.

(**f**) ten past six in the evening.

(**g**) quarter past eight in the evening.

(**h**) twenty five to seven in the morning.

(**i**) ten to five in the afternoon.

8.5 Time intervals

Example

Emma's train left Glasgow at 6.30 p.m. and arrived in Edinburgh at 7.25 p.m. How long did the journey take?

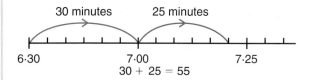

30 minutes   25 minutes

6·30   7·00   7·25

30 + 25 = 55

The journey takes 55 minutes.

Exercise 8.5

1 A train left Edinburgh at 2 p.m. and arrived in London at 6 p.m.
How long did the journey take?

2 Leslie started her lunch break at 12.10 p.m. and finished at 12.30 p.m.
How long did the break last?

3 Ari walked to the shops.
He left the house at 1.05 p.m. and arrived at 1.50 p.m.
How long did his journey take?

4 Period 5 at Aston Academy starts at 12.45 p.m. and ends at 1.20 p.m.
How long does it last?

5 Michael started his homework at 7 p.m.
He thought it would take 40 minutes.
When should he finish?

6 Rachel is watching a 30 minute comedy programme.
It started at 7.30 p.m.
When will it finish?

7 Ged's paper round takes 40 minutes.
He started at 7.10 a.m.
When should he finish?

8 Look at the TV page below.

BBC 1		**BBC 2**	
5.45	Evening news	5.30	Streets
6.30	Local news	6.00	King of the Comedy
6.50	Weather	6.30	Fluffy the Piano Player
6.55	Holiday UK	7.15	Civil War
7.20	*Film:* Lord of the Wings	8.30	News Tonight
10.30	Al and Trace	9.30	*Film:* Mr Beads
11.00	Late night topic	10.55	Film Diary

(**a**) What time does *Holiday UK* start?

(**b**) What time does *Film Diary* start?

(**c**) How long does *King of the Comedy* last?

(**d**) How long does the *Evening News* last?

(**e**) Which film lasts longest?

(**f**) Sam wants to record *King of the Comedy* and *Civil War*.
How much time will this take up on his video tape?

9 Look at the bus timetable below.

Carchester	3.25
Shelby	3.38
Finaburgh	3.42
Aberton	3.55
Colferry	4.10

(**a**) What time does the bus arrive in Finaburgh?

(**b**) What time does the bus arrive in Aberton?

(**c**) How long does the journey from Carchester to Shelby take?

(**d**) How long does the whole journey take?

8.6 Time intervals over noon

A train leaves Edinburgh at 11.30 a.m. and arrives in Berwick on Tweed at 12.15 p.m. How long does the journey last?

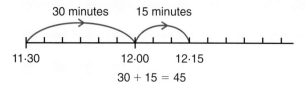

30 + 15 = 45

The journey lasts 45 minutes.

Exercise 8.6

1 A film started at 11 a.m. and finished at 1 p.m.
How long did the film last?

2 A flight left Glasgow at 10 a.m. and arrived in Athens at 4 p.m.
How long did the flight last?

3 Bethany started school at 9 a.m. and finished at 3.30 p.m.
How long was she at school?

4 A flight to Barcelona lasts three hours.
If the plane leaves Glasgow at 11 a.m., when should it arrive?

5 Look at the timetable below.

Carchester	11.33	11.53	12.40
Shelby	11.46	12.06	12.53
Fintown	11.50	12.10	
Aberton	12.03	12.23	
Colferry	12.18		

(**a**) At what times do the buses leave from Carchester?
(**b**) How long does the journey from Fintown
to Colferry last?
(**c**) What time should the 11.53 bus from Carchester
arrive in Colferry?
(**d**) Jonathan arrives at the bus stop in Carchester
at five to twelve.
How long does he have to wait until the next bus?

8.7 The calendar

30 days has September, April, June and November
All the rest have 31
Except February with 28 days clear
And 29 in each leap year.

OCTOBER

M	T	W	Th	F	S	S
			1	2	3	4	5
6	7	8	9	10	11	12
13	14	15	16	17	18	19
20	21	22	23	24	25	26
27	28	29	30	31		

1 year is 365 days or 366 days in a leap year.

1 year is 52 weeks approximately.

1 year is 12 months.

THE   No.452
GAZETTE
4/6/04   4th June 2004   35p

Exercise 8.7

1 Copy and complete this list of months.

January
April
June
August
November

2 How many days has
   (**a**) March   (**b**) June   (**c**) September
   (**d**) October   (**e**) December   (**f**) May?

3 Write the months which have passed from the start of the year to

(**a**)

MARCH

M	T	W	Th	F	S	S
1	2	3	4	5	6	7
8	9	10	11	12	13	14
15	16	17	18	19	20	21
22	23	24	25	26	27	28
29	30	31				

(**b**)

JULY

M	T	W	Th	F	S	S
			1	2	3	4	5	6
7	8	9	10	11	12	13
14	15	16	17	18	19	20
21	22	23	24	25	26	27
28	29	30	31			

4 Write the months which are still to come after the following months until the end of the year.

(**a**)

NOVEMBER

M	T	W	Th	F	S	S
	1	2	3	4	5	6
7	8	9	10	11	12	13
14	15	16	17	18	19	20
21	22	23	24	25	26	27
28	29	30				

(**b**)

AUGUST

M	T	W	Th	F	S	S
				1	2	3
4	5	6	7	8	9	10
11	12	13	14	15	16	17
18	19	20	21	22	23	24
25	26	27	28	29	30	31

5 Say whether each of these statements is true or false:
   (**a**) March has 31 days.   (**b**) August comes before October.
   (**c**) February is the shortest month.   (**d**) June has 31 days.
   (**e**) May comes before March.
   (**f**) There are 90 days altogether in April, May and June.

6 Write these dates in full.

    (**a**) 6/7/04   (**b**) 25/11/03   (**c**) 28/2/03

7 Write these dates using digits.

    (**a**) 4th April 2002   (**b**) 10th August 2004

    (**c**) 21st December 2004   (**d**) 12th January 2005

8 Use the calendar page to answer these questions.

    (**a**) What date is the first Monday in June?

    (**b**) What date is the third Wednesday?

    (**c**) What day will the 11th June be?

    (**d**) What day will the 24th June be?

    (**e**) What date is the last Friday in June?

			JUNE			
M	T	W	Th	F	S	S
	1	2	3	4	5	
7	8	9	10	11		
14	15	16	17			
21	22	23				
28	29	30				

9 Use the calendar pages to answer these questions.

    (**a**) How many Mondays are in September?

    (**b**) On what day is the 5th October?

    (**c**) On what day is the 20th September?

    (**d**) What are the dates of the Saturdays in November?

    (**e**) What date will be one week after the 26th November?

    (**f**) What is the date of the first Tuesday in December?

    (**g**) Robert is going on holiday for two weeks.
         If he leaves on the 16th October, on what date will he return?

    (**h**) Rachel's birthday is on the 2nd September.
         Her sister's birthday is one week earlier.
         When is her sister's birthday?

10 How many months are in:

(**a**) 3 years   (**b**) 4 years   (**c**) 6 years?

11 Approximately how many weeks are in:

(**a**) 2 years   (**b**) 3 years   (**c**) 4 years?

Review exercise 8

1 Write the times shown on these clocks:

(**a**) 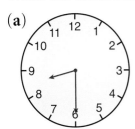   (**b**) 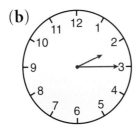   (**c**)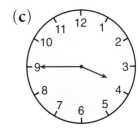

(**d**) 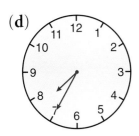   (**e**) 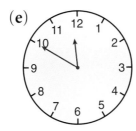   (**f**)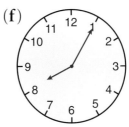

2 Draw the display of a **digital** clock showing these times.

(**a**) twenty five past eight.   (**b**) quarter past two.

(**c**) quarter to twelve.   (**d**) ten to nine.

3 Write these times using a.m. or p.m.

(**a**) half past three in the afternoon.

(**b**) ten to eleven in the morning.

(**c**) twenty past seven in the evening.

(**d**) twenty five to one in the afternoon.

4 A train left Edinburgh at 2 p.m. and arrived in Inverness at 6.30 p.m. How long did the journey take?

5 A film started at 10 a.m. and finished at 1.15 p.m. How long did the film last?

6 How many days has:

(**a**) April   (**b**) December   (**c**) May   (**d**) August?

7 Write these dates in full:

(**a**) 22/4/04   (**b**) 15/8/04   (**c**) 17/10/03

8 How many months are in 2 years?

9 Use the calendar page to answer these questions.

APRIL

M	T	W	Th	F	S	S
			1	2	3	4
5	6	7	8	9	10	11
12	13	14	15	16	17	18
19	20	21	22	23	24	25
26	27	28	29	30		

(**a**) What date is the first Monday in April?

(**b**) How many Saturdays are there in April?

(**c**) What day will the 19th April be?

(**d**) What date is the last Saturday in April?

(**e**) Marnie goes on holiday on 10th April for one week.
On what date will she return?

(**f**) The first day of Rebecca's work experience was 13th April.
Her last day was 17th April.
How many days was she working?

Summary

Telling the time

half past five

quarter past eleven

quarter to seven

Digital clocks

Digital clocks tell the number of minutes past the hour.

a.m. and p.m.

Times in the morning are written using a.m.
Times in the afternoon and evening are written using p.m.

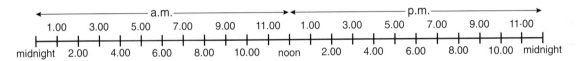

Time intervals

A film starts at 3.15 p.m. and finishes at 4.05 p.m.
How long does the film last?

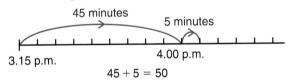

3.15 p.m.

4.00 p.m.

45 + 5 = 50

The film lasts 50 minutes.

The calendar

30 days has September, April, June and November.
  All the rest have 31.
Except February with 28 days clear.
  And 29 in each leap year.

1 year is 365 days or 366 days in a leap year.
1 year is 52 weeks approximately.
1 year is 12 months.
8th October 2004 can be written 8/10/04.

9 Information handling

In this chapter you will learn about ways of displaying information.

9.1 Reading tables

Information is often easier to read from a table.

The table shows meal prices at the Parrot Restaurant.

	Lunch	Dinner
1 course	£5.20	£7.50
2 courses	£6.80	£10.00
3 courses	£8.30	£12.00

Exercise 9.1

1 From the table above find the cost of:

(**a**) a 3 course lunch

(**b**) a 1 course dinner

(**c**) a 2 course lunch

(**d**) a 1 course lunch

(**e**) a 2 course dinner

(**f**) a 3 course dinner

2 Use the table above to write the cost for each person **and** find the total for each group:

(**a**) Mary   2 course lunch
     Liz   3 course lunch
     Sue   1 course lunch

(**b**) Sam   3 course dinner
     Ben   1 course dinner
     Tom   1 course dinner

3 The Table shows the start and finish times for the events at the Sunbay Resort.

	Start	Finish
Swimming	10.00 a.m.	10.30 a.m.
Diving	2.20 p.m.	4.00 p.m.
Football	4.30 p.m.	6.00 p.m.
Talent show	8.00 p.m.	9.30 p.m.

(**a**) What starts at 4.30 p.m.?

(**b**) How long is the diving?

(**c**) What finishes at 9.30 p.m.?

(**d**) When does the football end?

(**e**) When does the swimming start?

(**f**) When does the diving start?

(**g**) How long is the talent show?

(**h**) What finishes at 4.00 p.m.?

4 The table shows ferry prices to Whitsea Island.

	Adult	Child	Senior citizen
Single fare	£3	£2	£2
Return fare	£5	£3.50	£3.50

Find the cost of:

(**a**) an adult single fare
(**b**) a child return fare
(**c**) a senior citizen return fare
(**d**) an adult return fare
(**e**) 2 senior citizen and 3 adult return fares
(**f**) 2 adult and 4 child single fares.

5 The table shows ferry times for Whitsea Island.

Leave	Green Harbour	9.00	10.15	12.00	1.30	3.00	6.00
Arrive	Whitsea Island	9.45	11.00	12.45	2.15	3.45	6.45

(**a**) When does the 10.15 boat arrive in Whitsea Island?
(**b**) At what time does the last boat leave Green Harbour?
(**c**) When does the last ferry arrive at Whitsea Island?
(**d**) How long does the journey last?

6 The table shows interhouse competition points.

	Wallace	Fleming	Burns
Football	15	8	11
Chess	5	8	12
Netball	12	15	6

(**a**) How many points did Wallace house score for football?
(**b**) How many points did Burns house score for chess?
(**c**) Which house won at netball?
(**d**) Which house won the chess?
(**e**) How many points did Fleming house score for netball?
(**f**) Add up the points for each house.
   Which house won the competition?

7 Susan is checking her stock of packaged sandwiches. Her figures are in the table.

How many are:

	Twin packs	Triple packs
Cheese	8	5
Ham	20	12
Chicken	12	8

(**a**) twin packs of ham
(**b**) triple packs of chicken
(**c**) triple packs of cheese
(**d**) twin packs of chicken
(**e**) triple packs of ham
(**f**) twin packs of cheese?

8 The table shows favourite food choices for S1 classes.

	Curry	Chinese	Pizza	Burgers
1B1	8	12	5	2
1F1	3	8	16	0
1W1	10	9	6	3

How many chose:

(**a**) pizza in 1F1   (**b**) curry in 1W1   (**c**) burgers in 1B1

(**d**) Chinese in 1B1   (**e**) burgers in 1F1   (**f**) curry in 1B1?

9.2 Drawing tables

Roger is checking his cake stock.
He puts the information into a table.

Cream slices	Doughnuts	Jam tarts	Swiss buns	Eccles cakes
16	25	18	8	12

Exercise 9.2

W You need Worksheets **9.1** and **9.2** for questions **1** to **10**.

11 Copy and complete the table for the paper stock.

A4 Paper			A5 Paper
A4 Paper	A4 Paper		A5 Paper
A4 Paper	A3 Paper		A5 Paper
A4 Paper	A3 Paper	A3 Paper	
A4 Paper	A3 Paper	A3 Paper	
A4 Paper	A3 Paper	A3 Paper	

	A3	A4	A5
White	4		
Coloured			
Card			

12 Make a table for the shoe stock.

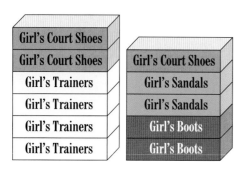

9.3 Pictographs

This **pictograph** shows the number of hours of sunshine during one week in December.

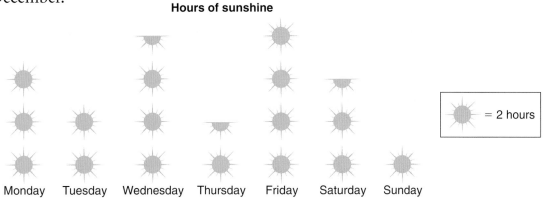

Saturday had 5 hours of sunshine.
Friday had the **most** hours of sunshine.
Sunday had the **least** number of hours.

Exercise 9.3

1 From the pictograph above, how many hours of sunshine were there on
   (**a**) Monday   (**b**) Wednesday   (**c**) Thursday
   (**d**) Tuesday   (**e**) Sunday   (**f**) Friday?

2 The pictograph shows the hours of sunshine in one week.
   (**a**) Which was the sunniest day?
   (**b**) Which two days had the same number of hours of sunshine?
   (**c**) Write the number of hours of sunshine for each day.

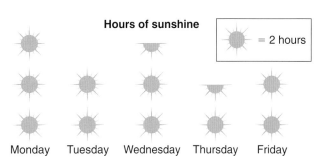

3 The pictograph shows the number of people waiting at the doctor's each hour.
   (**a**) How many were waiting at 8 a.m.
   (**b**) When is the busiest time?
   (**c**) When is the quietest time?
   (**d**) In total, how many people were waiting?

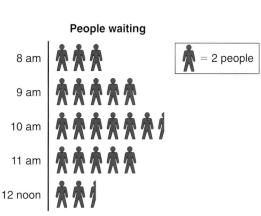

4 The pictograph shows how many of each kind of cake were sold.

   (**a**) How many jam sponges were sold?

   (**b**) How many chocolate cakes were sold?

   (**c**) What is the most popular cake?

   (**d**) Which is the least popular?

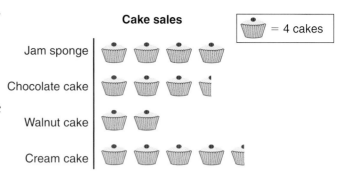

5 Six friends are saving for a holiday.

   (**a**) Who has saved the most?

   (**b**) How much has Sam saved?

   (**c**) How much has Sarah saved?

   (**d**) Who has saved the least money?

   (**e**) Tom needs £95 for the holiday. How much more does he need to save?

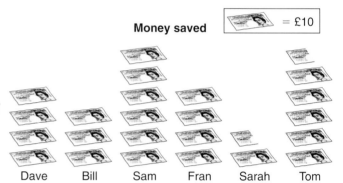

6 A travel company sells holidays to Hawaii.

   (**a**) How many were sold in May?

   (**b**) In which month did they sell the most?

   (**c**) Which month was the quietest?

   (**d**) In which month did they sell 24 holidays?

7 The pictograph shows the attendance at the school prom each year.

   (**a**) How many went in 2002?

   (**b**) Which year was most popular?

   (**c**) In which year did 110 go?

   (**d**) How many more went in 2003 than in 2004?

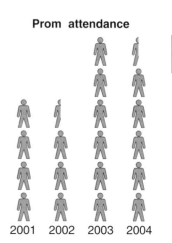

8 A cinema has recorded ticket sales.

(**a**) Which night is the busiest?

(**b**) Which is the quietest night?

(**c**) How many tickets were sold on Tuesday?

(**d**) On which night did they sell 350 tickets?

(**e**) How many tickets were sold in total?

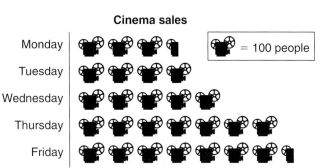

Cinema sales

9.4 Reading bar graphs

This **bar graph** shows the ways pupils in 1F2 travel to school.

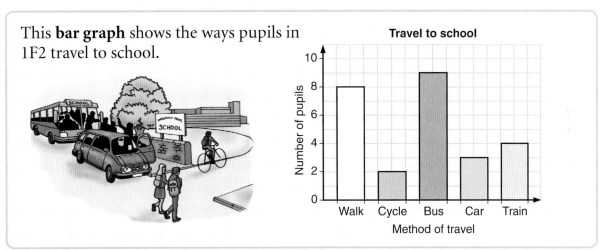

Exercise 9.4

1 From the bar graph above:

(**a**) How do most people travel to school?

(**b**) Which is the least common way to travel?

(**c**) How many travel by bus?

(**d**) How many travel by train?

2 The bar graph shows the six favourite subjects in a survey of 48 pupils.

(**a**) How many chose History?

(**b**) How many chose Music?

(**c**) What is the least popular subject?

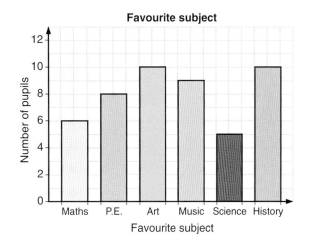

3 The bar graph shows the points scored in a
swimming competition.
- (**a**) Who won the competition?
- (**b**) Which team was last?
- (**c**) How many points did the Urchins score?
- (**d**) By how much did the Dolphins beat
the Sharks?

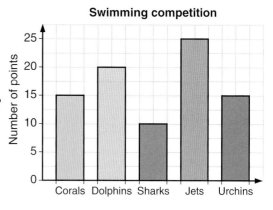

4 For a charity appeal Alton High School raised
money in several ways.
- (**a**) Which method raised most money?
- (**b**) Which method was least successful?
- (**c**) How much did the talent show raise?
- (**d**) Which event raised £20?
- (**e**) How much money was raised in total?

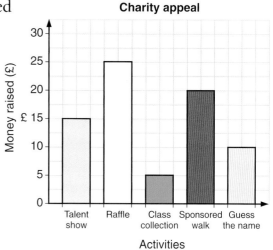

5 A car rental firm charts its rentals in one week.
- (**a**) Which is the most popular car?
- (**b**) Which is the least popular?
- (**c**) How many estate cars were rented?
- (**d**) Which type of car was rented 10 times?
- (**e**) How many cars were rented in total?

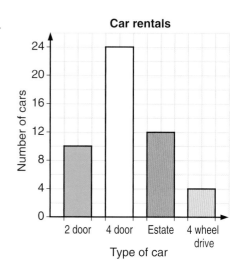

6 The bar graph shows the number of hours worked by 6 employees.

(**a**) How long does Kay work?

(**b**) Who works the longest?

(**c**) Who works the least number of hours?

(**d**) Who works 4 hours each week?

(**e**) What was the total number of hours worked?

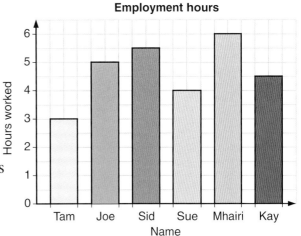

7 The bar graph shows goals for and against four football teams.

(**a**) How many goals did Rovers score?

(**b**) How many goals were scored against United?

(**c**) Which team scored 6 goals?

(**d**) Which teams had 3 goals scored against them?

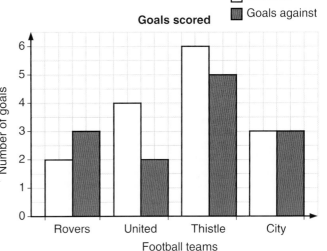

8 The school librarian has charted the books taken out by S2 classes.

(**a**) Which class took out least books?

(**b**) Which class took out the most?

(**c**) In which class did the boys borrow 25 books?

(**d**) In which class did the girls borrow 15 books?

(**e**) Who borrows most books, boys or girls?

(**f**) What is the total number of books borrowed?

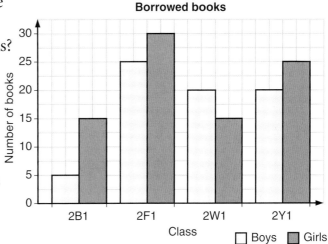

9.5 Drawing bar graphs

When drawing bar graphs remember
- number the vertical axis evenly
- label each axis
- name the graph

Example

Draw a bar graph to show this information about group sizes.

Group	A	B	C	D	E
Size	8	7	3	9	6

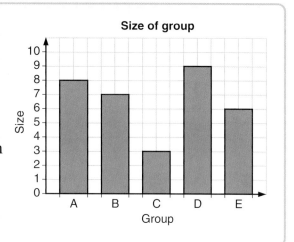

Exercise 9.5

W You need Worksheets **9.3** to **9.6** for questions **1** to **8**.

9 Draw a bar graph of this information.

Hotel	Rio	Sole	Lara	Stella	Luna
Employees	12	9	15	20	12

10 Draw a bar graph of this information.

Name	Fred	Bill	Bridget	Sandra	Colin	Brian
Hours worked	8	7	10	5	5	9

Review exercise 9

1 The table shows the prices of plant trays.

Tray size	6	12	18	24
Price	£2.40	£4.50	£6.50	£8.50

(a) How much does a 12 plant tray cost?
(b) How many plants could you buy for £6·50?
(c) Susan bought two 24 plant trays.
   How much would she pay?

2 The table shows the prices on a drinks machine.

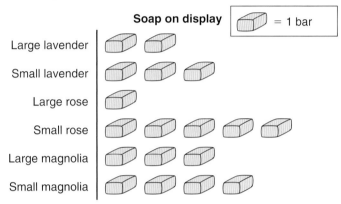

	Water	Kola	Lift	Soda
500 ml	£0.55	£0.70	£0.70	£0.65
1 litre	£1	£1·30	£1·30	£1·20

(**a**) How much is a 500 ml bottle of Soda?

(**b**) How much is a 1 litre bottle of water?

(**c**) Which two drinks cost exactly the same?

(**d**) Frosini buys a 500 ml bottle of Kola and a 1 litre bottle of Lift. How much is this?

3 Use Colin's soap display to copy and complete the table.

	Lavender	Rose	Magnolia
Large			
Small			

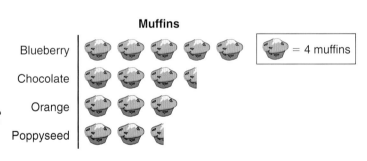

Soap on display   = 1 bar

Large lavender
Small lavender
Large rose
Small rose
Large magnolia
Small magnolia

4 The pictograph shows the sales of muffins in the baker's.

(**a**) How many chocolate muffins were sold?

(**b**) Which is the most popular?

(**c**) Which is the least popular?

(**d**) The baker sold 12 of which kind of muffin?

Muffins

Blueberry
Chocolate
Orange
Poppyseed

= 4 muffins

5 The pictograph shows the number of pupils who chose school activities.

(**a**) How many chose cycling?

(**b**) Which is the most popular activity?

(**c**) Which activity did 15 pupils choose?

(**d**) Which is the least popular activity?

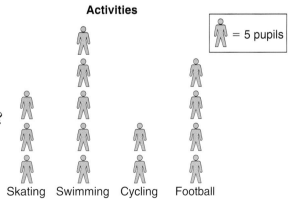

Activities

= 5 pupils

Skating   Swimming   Cycling   Football

6 The bar graph shows the use of a swimming
pool at five sessions during the day.

(**a**) Which is the most popular time?

(**b**) Which is the least popular time?

(**c**) How many people used the pool
between 1 p.m. and 2 p.m.?

(**d**) At what time were there 16 people in
the pool?

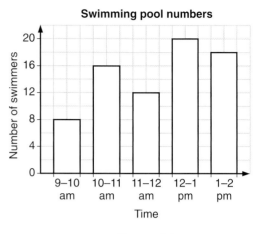

7 Mr McCormack draws a bar graph of the
number of pupils at his lunchtime chess club.

(**a**) Which is the most popular day?

(**b**) On what day did the fewest people come?

(**c**) On which day were there 8 pupils?

(**d**) How many attended on Thursday?

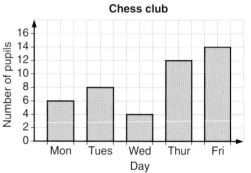

8 Use the table to copy and complete the bar graph.

Month	Nov	Dec	Jan	Feb	Mar
Temperature (°C)	11	10	8	9	12

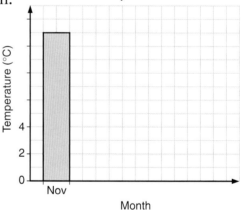

9 Class 1B2 grew seedlings in trays.
Use the table to copy and complete the bar graph.

Name	Ali	Kim	Fay	Sue	Kai
Seedlings grown	12	15	3	18	9

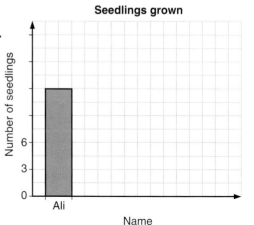

Summary

Tables

Information may be shown in a table.

	Small	Large
Peaches	3	4
Pineapple	2	5
Pears	2	1

Pictographs

Information may be shown in a pictograph.

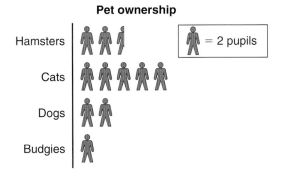

5 pupils own hamsters.

Bar graphs

Information may be shown in a bar graph.

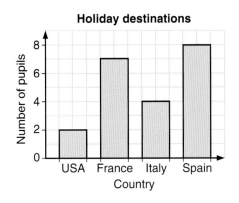

7 pupils went to France.

10 Equations

10.1 Addition

A letter can stand for an unknown number.

Example 1

If $x + 3 = 8$, what number is x?

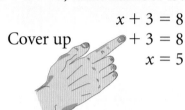

$$x + 3 = 8$$

Cover up

$$+ 3 = 8$$

$$x = 5$$

5 plus 3 equals 8

x must be 5

$x + 3 = 8$ is called an **equation**.

Example 2

Solve the equation $10 + p = 18$

$$10 + p = 18$$

Cover up

$$10 + = 18$$

$$p = 8$$

10 plus 8 equals 18

p must be 8

Exercise 10.1

1 Copy and complete:

(**a**) $x + 3 = 9$
$x =$

(**b**) $x + 5 = 7$
$x =$

(**c**) $12 + m = 13$
$m =$

(**d**) $q + 6 = 16$
$q =$

(**e**) $3 + f = 6$
$f =$

(**f**) $y + 1 = 23$
$y =$

2 Solve the equations:

(**a**) $x + 3 = 10$

(**b**) $y + 5 = 8$

(**c**) $7 + c = 9$

(**d**) $z + 10 = 20$

(**e**) $2 + x = 6$

(**f**) $y + 4 = 8$

(**g**) $x + 2 = 17$

(**h**) $4 + z = 11$

(**i**) $6 + c = 12$

(**j**) $11 + x = 22$

(**k**) $y + 20 = 30$

(**l**) $z + 8 = 15$

(**m**) $y + 20 = 50$

(**n**) $5 + m = 25$

(**o**) $y + 12 = 18$

(**p**) $z + 21 = 30$

(**q**) $x + 7 = 16$

(**r**) $x + 8 = 21$

(**s**) $6 + p = 23$

(**t**) $16 + y = 21$

(**u**) $z + 22 = 31$

(**v**) $r + 30 = 60$

(**w**) $z + 25 = 75$

(**x**) $50 + y = 85$

3 Solve:
(**a**) $y + 30 = 43$ (**b**) $x + 16 = 31$ (**c**) $c + 15 = 29$
(**d**) $14 + m = 25$ (**e**) $g + 11 = 33$ (**f**) $x + 23 = 30$
(**g**) $125 + x = 200$ (**h**) $y + 400 = 500$ (**i**) $j + 55 = 100$
(**j**) $m + 8 = 36$ (**k**) $z + 16 = 32$ (**l**) $45 + s = 105$
(**m**) $x + 13 = 40$ (**n**) $36 + y = 50$ (**o**) $x + 55 = 70$

10.2 Subtraction

Example
Solve the equations
(**a**)
Cover up
$$x - 4 = 6$$
$$- 4 = 6$$
$$x = 10$$
10 minus 4 equals 6
x must be 10

(**b**)
Cover up
$$17 - y = 11$$
$$17 - = 11$$
$$y = 6$$
17 minus 6 equals 11
y must be 6

Exercise 10.2

1 Copy and complete:
(**a**) $x - 4 = 3$ (**b**) $12 - y = 10$ (**c**) $6 - p = 5$
   $x =$ $y =$ $p =$
(**d**) $a - 5 = 4$ (**e**) $m - 7 = 5$ (**f**) $8 - s = 2$
   $a =$ $m =$ $s =$

2 Solve the equations:
(**a**) $x - 5 = 3$ (**b**) $y - 10 = 5$ (**c**) $20 - z = 15$
(**d**) $30 - m = 20$ (**e**) $z - 2 = 10$ (**f**) $y - 3 = 7$
(**g**) $5 - x = 4$ (**h**) $20 - y = 10$ (**i**) $s - 1 = 9$
(**j**) $m - 4 = 16$ (**k**) $r - 20 = 30$ (**l**) $y - 3 = 13$
(**m**) $50 - y = 40$ (**n**) $x - 5 = 1$ (**o**) $10 - x = 8$
(**p**) $r - 6 = 14$ (**q**) $17 - p = 16$ (**r**) $30 - z = 25$
(**s**) $45 - y = 30$ (**t**) $x - 11 = 9$ (**u**) $a - 4 = 3$
(**v**) $z - 4 = 8$ (**w**) $16 - f = 16$ (**x**) $x - 5 = 7$

10.3 Equations – addition and subtraction
Exercise 10.3

1 Solve the equations:

(a) $x + 7 = 20$ (b) $y + 3 = 11$ (c) $4 - y = 3$

(d) $b - 3 = 0$ (e) $6 + z = 10$ (f) $10 + m = 25$

(g) $x - 5 = 15$ (h) $24 - m = 20$ (i) $30 - x = 26$

(j) $y + 4 = 17$ (k) $5 + x = 35$ (l) $z + 11 = 31$

(m) $45 - y = 35$ (n) $a - 7 = 0$ (o) $a + 6 = 22$

(p) $m + 45 = 65$ (q) $11 + y = 11$ (r) $f + 40 = 75$

2 Solve:

(a) $y - 3 = 12$ (b) $15 - x = 8$ (c) $z - 4 = 25$

(d) $3 + p = 14$ (e) $x + 24 = 36$ (f) $y + 15 = 35$

(g) $x + 10 = 110$ (h) $35 - x = 20$ (i) $y - 2 = 18$

(j) $50 - y = 25$ (k) $x - 20 = 80$ (l) $x + 22 = 30$

10.4 Solving problems

Example

Susan has x pounds in each piggy bank.
In total she has £15.
Find the value of x.

$x + x + x = 15$
$\quad\quad x = 5$ $\boxed{5 + 5 + 5 = 15}$

There is £5 in each piggy bank.

Exercise 10.4

Find the value of x:

1

Total £12 $\boxed{x + x + x + x = 12}$

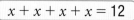

2

Total £20

3

Total £18

4

Total £30

5

Total 32 sweets

6

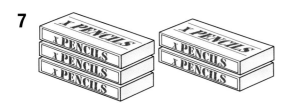

Total 40 sweets

7

Total 40 pencils

8

Total 27 pencils

9

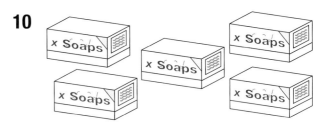

Total 24 soaps

10

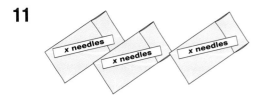

Total 25 soaps

11

Total 18 needles

12

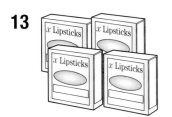

Total 20 spice jars

13

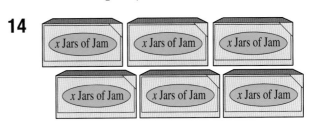

Total 16 lipsticks

14

Total 36 jars of jam

10.5 Multiplication

3*y* means **3 multiplied by *y***, or **3 × *y***
7*m* means **7 multiplied by *m***, or **7 × *m***

Examples
Solve the equations (**a**) $4x = 20$ (**b**) $3m = 21$

(**a**)
  Cover up

  $4x = 20$
  $4\bullet = 20$ ⟨ 4 times 5 equals 20 ⟩
  $x = 5$

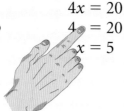

(**b**)
  Cover up

  $3m = 21$
  $3\bullet = 21$ ⟨ 3 times 7 equals 21 ⟩
  $m = 7$

Exercise 10.5

1 Copy and complete:

(**a**) $4a = 12$ (**b**) $6c = 60$ (**c**) $5x = 25$
   $a =$ $c =$ $x =$

(**d**) $4m = 8$ (**e**) $2f = 14$ (**f**) $3s = 9$
   $m =$ $f =$ $s =$

2 Solve each equation:

(**a**) $5y = 10$ (**b**) $4m = 16$ (**c**) $10p = 50$
(**d**) $6y = 18$ (**e**) $8x = 40$ (**f**) $7x = 49$
(**g**) $2p = 20$ (**h**) $5y = 50$ (**i**) $9z = 36$
(**j**) $4x = 28$ (**k**) $6y = 42$ (**l**) $3z = 90$
(**m**) $10z = 70$ (**n**) $10y = 60$ (**o**) $7x = 7$
(**p**) $10y = 30$ (**q**) $8y = 64$ (**r**) $9y = 81$
(**s**) $4z = 4$ (**t**) $5z = 30$ (**u**) $2y = 100$
(**v**) $8p = 24$ (**w**) $10y = 100$ (**x**) $5m = 0$

Review exercise 10

1 Solve each equation:

(**a**) $x + 5 = 11$ (**b**) $y + 3 = 12$ (**c**) $7 + z = 16$

(**d**) $p + 10 = 17$ (**e**) $20 + m = 32$ (**f**) $12 + y = 25$

(**g**) $x + 20 = 35$ (**h**) $z + 25 = 50$ (**i**) $50 + y = 150$

2 Solve:

(**a**) $y - 5 = 15$ (**b**) $x - 3 = 17$ (**c**) $20 - m = 18$

(**d**) $15 - y = 14$ (**e**) $21 - x = 18$ (**f**) $z - 10 = 20$

(**g**) $y - 3 = 11$ (**h**) $z - 20 = 30$ (**i**) $x - 25 = 75$

3 Solve:

(**a**) $6y = 36$ (**b**) $7y = 42$ (**c**) $3m = 24$

(**d**) $10z = 90$ (**e**) $4x = 36$ (**f**) $5m = 20$

(**g**) $8x = 72$ (**h**) $11y = 11$ (**i**) $20x = 80$

4 Solve:

(**a**) $y + 20 = 30$ (**b**) $x - 9 = 11$ (**c**) $15 - z = 12$

(**d**) $5m = 10$ (**e**) $3z = 33$ (**f**) $4 + p = 12$

(**g**) $z + 15 = 22$ (**h**) $8z = 240$ (**i**) $9 - x = 8$

(**j**) $21 - y = 19$ (**k**) $x - 4 = 9$ (**l**) $7y = 35$

5 Find the value of y:

(**a**)

Total £27

b)

Total 32 pencils

Summary

A letter can stand for an unknown number.

Solve $x + 5 = 11$

$$x + 5 = 11$$
$$+ 5 = 11$$
$$x = 6$$

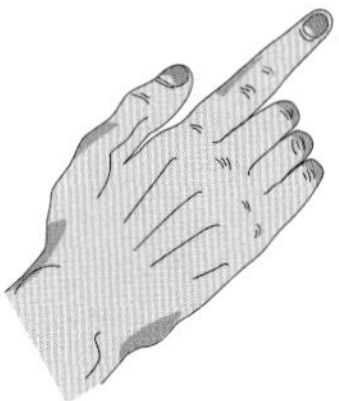

Solve $12 - p = 3$

$$12 - p = 3$$
$$12 - = 3$$
$$p = 9$$

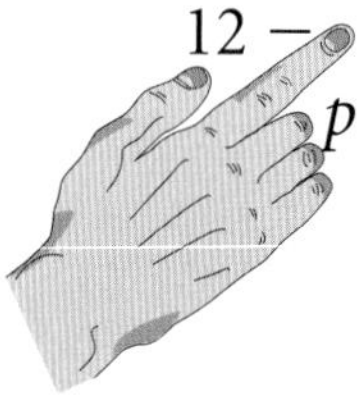

Solve $8r = 24$

$$8r = 24$$
$$8 = 24$$
$$r = 3$$

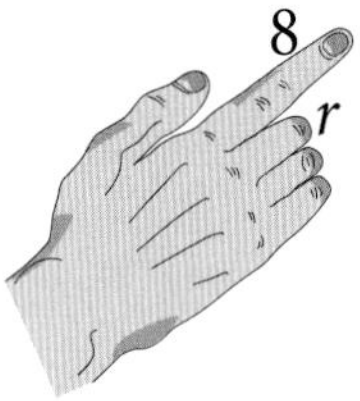

$8r$ means $8 \times r$

11 Coordinates

In this chapter you will learn how to read and plot coordinates.

11.1 Reading coordinates

The position of a point may be described by its **coordinates**.
The horizontal line is called the **x-axis** and the vertical line is called the **y-axis**.
The point where the x-axis and y-axis meet is called the **origin**, **O**.

Examples
From the origin, to the point A count 2 along then 1 up.
A has coordinates (2, 1)
This is written as **A(2, 1)**
The other coordinates are **B(1, 5)** and **C(4, 3)**.

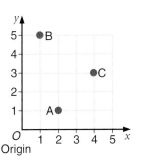

Exercise 11.1

1 Write the coordinates of each point.

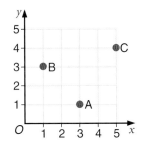

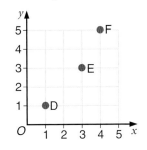

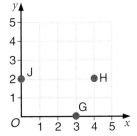

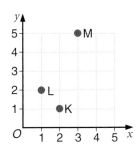

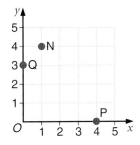

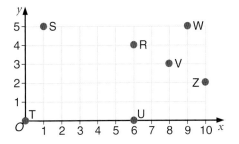

W You need Worksheet **11.1** for questions **2** and **3**.

11.2 Plotting coordinates

Marking a point on a coordinate diagram is called **plotting** a point.

To plot $(3, 7)$, start from the origin, count along 3 then up 7.

Exercise 11.2

W You need Worksheets **11.2** and **11.3** for questions **1** to **8**.

Number the lines carefully, as shown.

9 (a) Copy the diagram.
   (b) Plot the points A$(2, 5)$, B$(5, 2)$, C$(3, 0)$ and D$(0, 3)$.
   (c) Join A, B, C and D.
       What shape is ABCD?

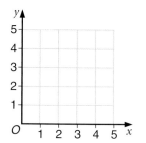

10 (a) Copy the diagram.
   (b) Plot the points E$(2, 1)$, F$(5, 1)$ and G$(3, 3)$.
   (c) Join E, F and G.
       What shape is EFG?

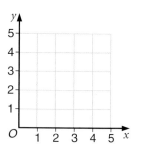

11 (a) Copy the diagram.
   (b) Plot the points H$(0, 2)$, I$(2, 0)$ and J$(4, 2)$.
   (c) Plot point K to make HIJK a square.
   (d) Write the coordinates of K.

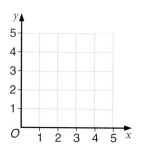

W You need Worksheet **11.4** for question **12**.

Review exercise 11

1 Write the coordinates of each point:

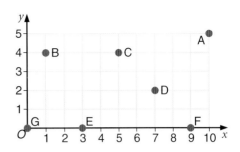

2 Look at the diagram shown.
Write the coordinates of:

(**a**) the bank   (**b**) the toy shop
(**c**) the post office   (**d**) the butcher
(**e**) the baker   (**f**) the candlestick maker
(**g**) the doctor   (**h**) the dentist
(**i**) the vet   (**j**) the school
(**k**) the police station (**l**) the supermarket
(**m**) the park

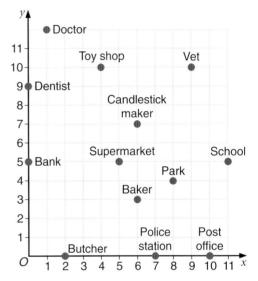

3 Copy the diagram.
Plot the points A(2, 3), B(4, 0), C(0, 4),
D(8, 4), E(5, 5) and F(10, 4).

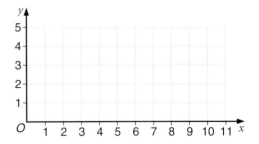

4 Copy the diagram.

(**a**) Plot the points P(4, 1), Q(0, 3),
R(1, 5) and S(5, 3).

(**b**) Join the points.
What shape is PQRS?

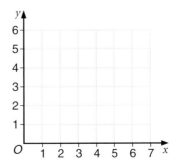

5 Copy the diagram.
Plot the points joining them in order and name the object.
$(4, 5)$ $(0, 2)$ $(5, 1)$ $(1, 5)$ $(2, 0)$ $(4, 5)$.

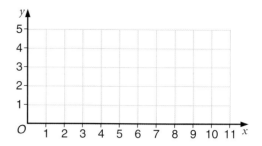

6 Copy the diagram.
  (a) Plot the points $P(3, 1)$, $Q(5, 3)$, $R(3, 5)$ and $S(1, 3)$.
  (b) Join the points.
     What shape is PQRS?

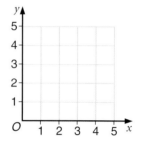

7 Copy the diagram.
  (a) Plot the points $A(8, 1)$, $B(0, 1)$ and $C(0, 4)$.
  (b) Plot D so that ABCD is a rectangle.
  (c) Write the coordinates of D.

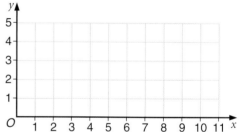

Summary

The position of a point is described by its **coordinates**.

The horizontal line is called the **x-axis** and the vertical line is called the **y-axis**.
The point where the x-axis and y-axis meet is called the **origin, O**.

A has coordinates $(3, 1)$.
  This is written as $A(3, 1)$.

B has coordinates $(2, 5)$.
  This is written as $B(2, 5)$.

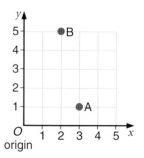

From the origin count **along** then **up**.

Marking points on a coordinate diagram is called **plotting** points.

12 Shape

In this chapter you will learn more about flat and solid shapes.

12.1 Shapes

Remember   These are **two-dimensional** or flat shapes.

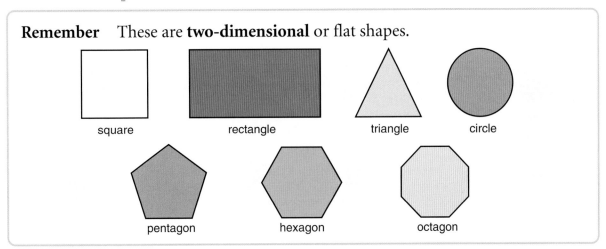

square   rectangle   triangle   circle

pentagon   hexagon   octagon

Exercise 12.1

1 Copy this table and complete the number of sides for each shape.

Shape	Hexagon	Triangle	Square	Octagon	Pentagon	Rectangle
Number of sides						

2 Write the names of the two-dimensional shapes you can see in each diagram.

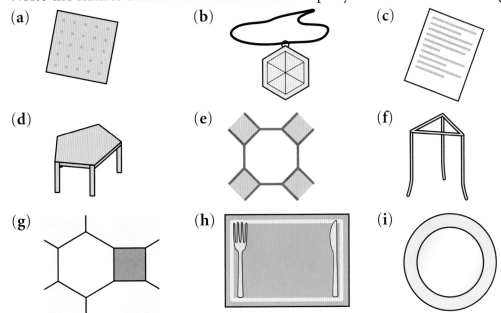

(a)

(b)

(c)

(d)

(e)

(f)

(g)

(h)

(i)

W You need Worksheets **12.1** and **12.2** for question **3**.

12.2 Squares and rectangles

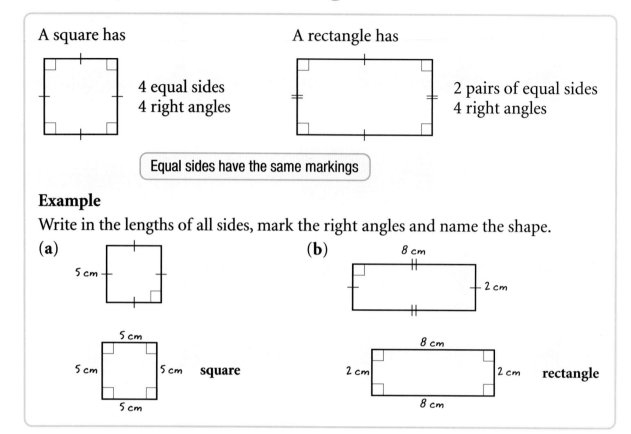

Example

Write in the lengths of all sides, mark the right angles and name the shape.

(a)

(b)

Exercise 12.2

W You need Worksheet **12.3** for question **1**.

12.3 Triangles

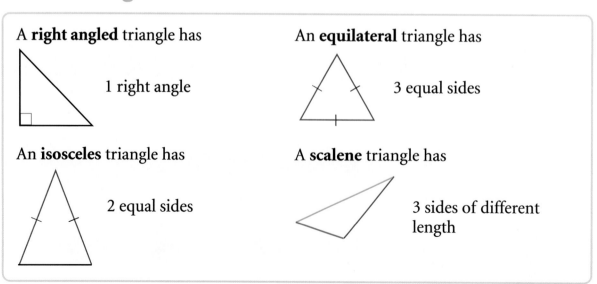

Exercise 12.3

1 Name each type of triangle. Choose from right angled, equilateral, isosceles or scalene

(**a**)

(**b**)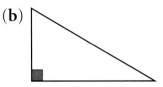

(**c**)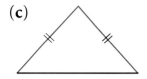

(**d**)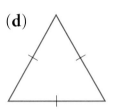

(**e**)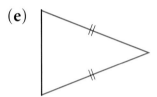

(**f**)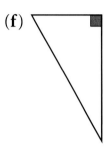

(**g**)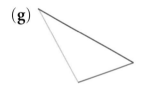

(**h**)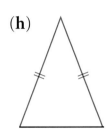

(**i**)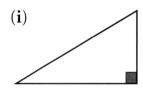

2 Name the type of triangle coloured:
(**a**) blue   (**b**) pink   (**c**) yellow
(**d**) green   (**e**) red   (**f**) brown.

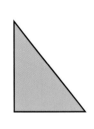 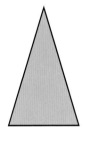 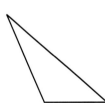

  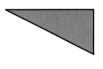

W You need Worksheet **12.4** for question **3**.

12.4 3D shapes

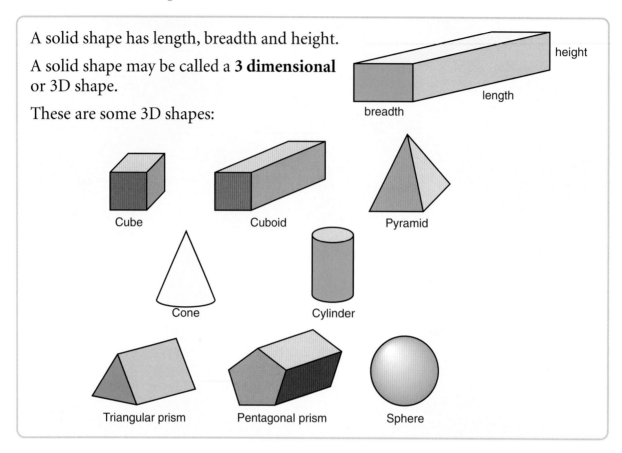

A solid shape has length, breadth and height.

A solid shape may be called a **3 dimensional** or 3D shape.

These are some 3D shapes:

Cube

Cuboid

Pyramid

Cone

Cylinder

Triangular prism

Pentagonal prism

Sphere

Exercise 12.4

1 Name each solid shape:

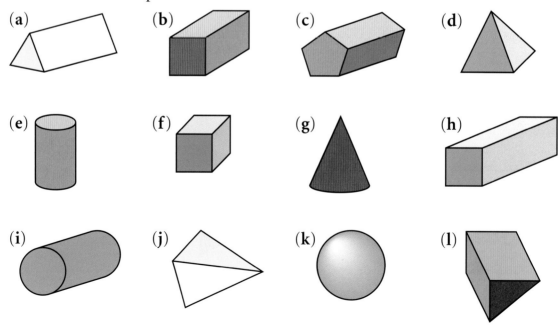

(a)

(b)

(c)

(d)

(e)

(f)

(g)

(h)

(i)

(j)

(k)

(l)

2 Name the 3 dimensional shape you can see in each diagram.

(**a**)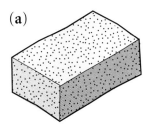

(**b**)

(**c**)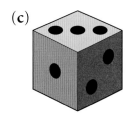

(**d**)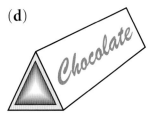

(**e**)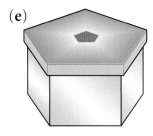

(**f**)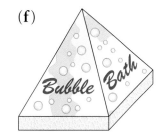

(**g**)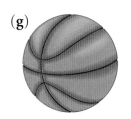

(**h**)

(**i**)

3 Massimo is playing with his building blocks.
Name the 3D shapes he has used for each tower.

(**a**)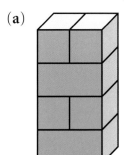

(**b**)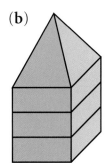

(**c**)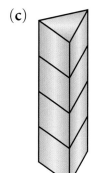

(**d**)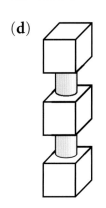

4 Carla makes sculptures using 3D shapes.
Which ones has she used for each sculpture?

(a)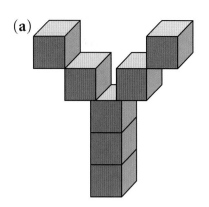

(b)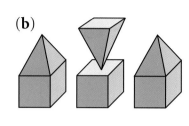

(c)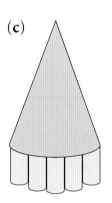

(d)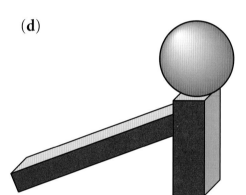

12.5 Vertices, edges and faces

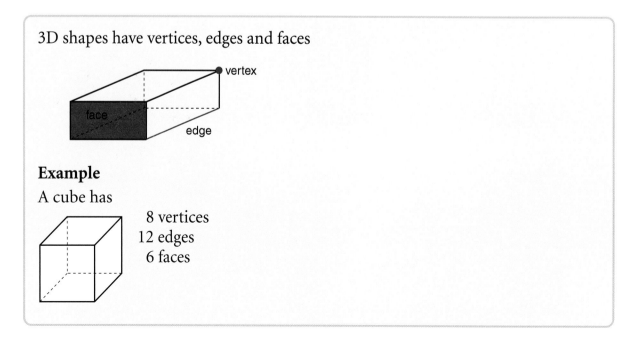

3D shapes have vertices, edges and faces

vertex

face

edge

Example

A cube has

8 vertices
12 edges
6 faces

Exercise 12.5

1 In each diagram, use the word vertex, edge or face to name the red part:

(**a**)   (**b**) 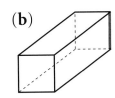   (**c**) 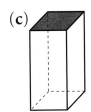   (**d**)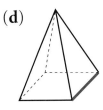

(**e**)   (**f**) 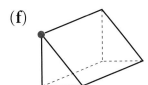   (**g**) 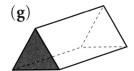   (**h**)

(**i**) 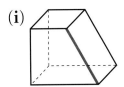   (**j**) 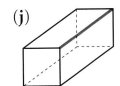   (**k**) 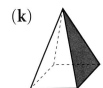   (**l**)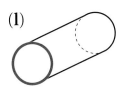

2 For each diagram, copy the table and complete the number of vertices, edges and faces.

(**a**)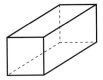

vertices	8
edges	
faces	

(**b**)

vertices	
edges	12
faces	

(**c**)

vertices	
edges	
faces	5

(**d**)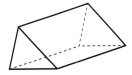

vertices	
edges	9
faces	

(**e**)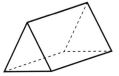

vertices	
edges	
faces	5

(**f**)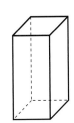

vertices	
edges	
faces	

(**g**)

vertices	
edges	
faces	

(**h**)

vertices	
edges	
faces	

3 Write whether each sentence is true or false.

(**a**) A cube has 8 vertices.

(**b**) A cuboid has 8 faces.

(**c**) The pyramid has 5 faces.

(**d**) The triangular prism has 10 edges.

(**e**) A cone has one vertex.

(**f**) A cylinder has 2 faces.

(**g**) A cube has 12 edges.

(**h**) The pyramid has 8 edges.

(**i**) The triangular prism has 6 vertices.

(**j**) A cuboid has 6 faces.

(**k**) A sphere has no vertices.

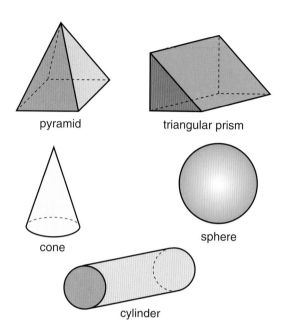

pyramid   triangular prism

cone   sphere

cylinder

Review exercise 12

1 Name each 2D shape.

(**a**)

(**b**)

(**c**)

(**d**)

2 How many sides has a:
(**a**) triangle
(**b**) square
(**c**) hexagon
(**d**) pentagon?

3 Copy the coordinate diagram.
Plot each set of points, join them up and name the shape.

(**a**) $(1, 6), (1, 10), (4, 7)$
(**b**) $(1, 3), (3, 1), (7, 5), (5, 7)$
(**c**) $(8, 6), (10, 8), (8, 10), (6, 8)$

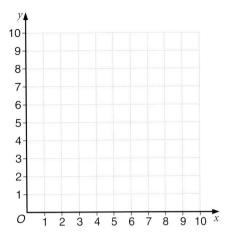

4 Copy each diagram. Write in the lengths of all sides, mark the right angle and name the shape.

(**a**)
4 cm

(**b**)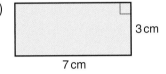
3 cm
7 cm

(**c**)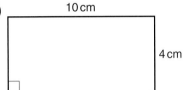
10 cm
4 cm

5 Name each type of triangle from the list: scalene, right angled, isosceles or equilateral.

(**a**)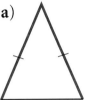

(**b**)

(**c**)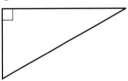

(**d**)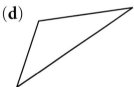

(**e**)

(**f**)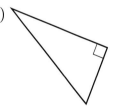

6 Copy the coordinate diagram.
Plot each set of points, join them up and name the type of triangle.

(**a**) $(1, 1), (4, 1), (4, 5)$
(**b**) $(1, 3), (1, 9), (2, 4)$
(**c**) $(5, 2), (9, 2), (7, 10)$

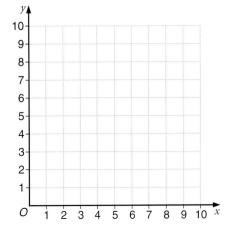

7 Name each 3D shape.

(a) 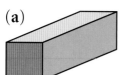   (b) 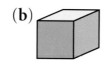   (c)    (d)

8 Name the red part as a vertex, edge or face.

(a)   (b) 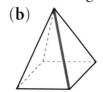   (c) 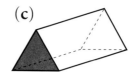   (d)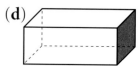

(e) 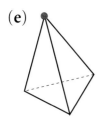   (f) 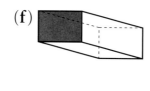   (g) 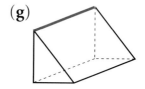   (h)

(i)    (j) 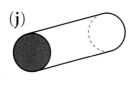   (k) 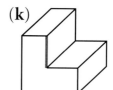   (l)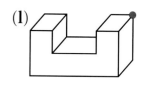

9 Copy and complete the table for each 3D shape.

(a)

vertices	8
edges	
faces	

(b)

vertices	
edges	
faces	

10 Write true or false for each sentence.

(a) A cube has 6 faces.

(b) A sphere has one edge.

(c) A triangular prism has 5 faces.

(d) A cylinder has 3 faces.

(e) A cube has 12 vertices.

Summary

2D shapes

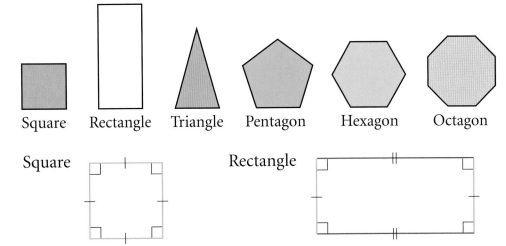

Square   Rectangle   Triangle   Pentagon   Hexagon   Octagon

Square   Rectangle

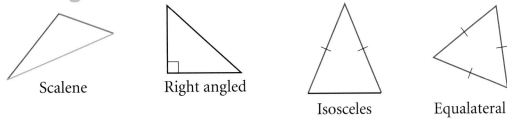

Triangles

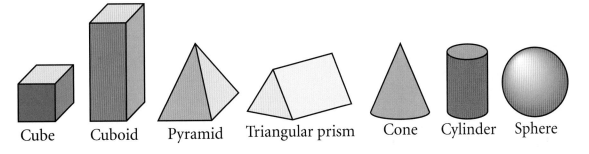

Scalene   Right angled

Isosceles   Equalateral

3D shapes

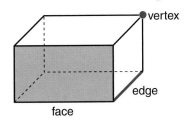

Cube   Cuboid   Pyramid   Triangular prism   Cone   Cylinder   Sphere

Vertices, edges and faces

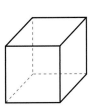

vertex

edge

face

A cube has 8 vertices
12 edges
6 faces

13 Problem solving

In this chapter you will practise problem solving.

Exercise 13.1

1 (**a**) Copy this numbered square.

1	2	3
4	5	6
7	8	9

(**b**) Use **four** of these ▭ rectangles to cover **eight** of the numbered squares. Leave number 5 uncovered.

(**c**) Which other number could be left uncovered?
What do you notice about these numbers?

2 Rab noticed a strange fact about the nine times table.
(**a**) Copy the table and complete the answer column.
(**b**) Add the digits in each answer to complete the table.
(**c**) What do you notice?

Number of digits

9 X 1	9	9 = 9
9 X 2	18	1 + 8 = 9
9 X 3	27	2 + 7 = 9
9 X 4	36	3 + 6 = 9
9 X 5	45	4 + 5 = 9
9 X 6	54	5 + 4 = 9
9 X 7	63	6 + 3 = 9
9 X 8	72	7 + 2 = 9
9 X 9	81	8 + 1 = 9

3 When Linda went into her maths classroom she saw that the teacher had not cleaned the blackboard.

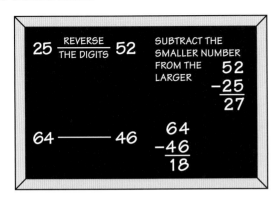

That looks interesting. I'll try it with some other numbers.

Eureka! All the answers...

(**a**) Follow the instructions on the blackboard for
(**i**) 26 (**ii**) 71 (**iii**) 45 (**iv**) 81.

(**b**) Choose your own number and follow the instructions.

(**c**) What was Linda's discovery?

4 You need A4 paper and a ruler and compasses.
This view of the Forth Road Bridge shows a **parabola**.
Follow these steps to draw a parabola.

Step 1

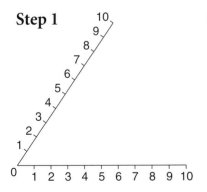

- Draw an angle with arms 10 cm long.
- Mark and number each centimetre along the arms.

Step 2

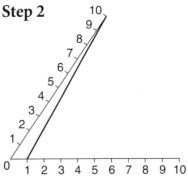

- Join point 1 on one arm to point 10 on the other.

Step 3

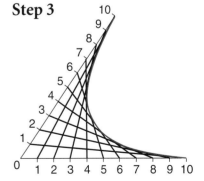

- Join points 2 to 9, 3 to 8 and so on.
- Draw the smooth curve shown by the red line.

The curve you have drawn is called the envelope of the lines.
This envelope is in the shape of a parabola.

5 Follow these steps to draw another envelope.

Step 1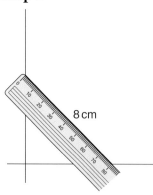

Step 2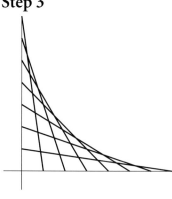

Step 3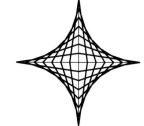

- Draw 2 lines each 16 cm long, which halve each other at right angles.

- In the top right-hand quarter of the diagram, draw a line 8 cm long as shown.

- Draw more lines each 8 cm long.

Step 4: Repeat Step 3 in each of the other quarters of your diagram. Draw the envelope of your lines.

This envelope is called an astroid.

6 You need square dot paper.
Some of the most beautiful buildings in the world are decorated with Islamic patterns.

Draw an Islamic pattern using the instructions below.

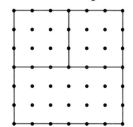

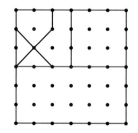

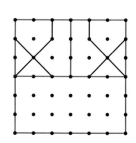

- Copy this diagram.

- Draw 3 lines in the top left square.

- Reflect in the line AB.

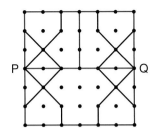

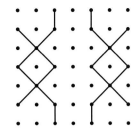

- Reflect in the line PQ.

- Redraw the pattern without the red lines.

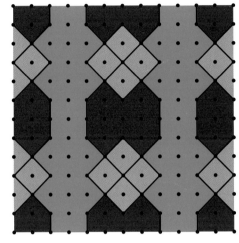

- Extend and colour the pattern.

7 Repeat the instructions to draw an Islamic pattern from each of the following.

(**a**) (**b**) (**c**) (**d**)

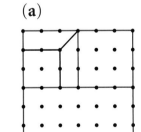 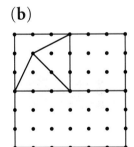 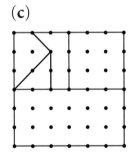 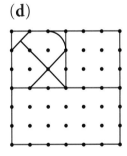

8 Repeat the instructions to draw your own Islamic pattern starting in the top left square with

(**a**) 3 lines (**b**) 4 lines.

Answers

Chapter 1

1 (b) 51   (c) 139   (d) 706   (e) 2780
  (f) 4244   (g) 6083   (h) 1002
  (i) three thousand one hundred and sixty two
  (j) five hundred and eighty one
  (k) two thousand and seventy nine
  (l) six hundred and twenty
  (m) five thousand and four
  (n) nine thousand eight hundred and six
2 (a) 32   (b) 217   (c) 604   (d) 410
  (e) 5123   (f) 6017   (g) 2008
3 (a) forty three
  (b) ninety
  (c) seven hundred and fourteen
  (d) eight hundred and twenty five
  (e) five hundred and seventy
  (f) three hundred and five
  (g) two thousand one hundred and seventy four
  (h) two thousand and six
  (i) six thousand and fifty
  (j) three thousand two hundred
  (k) one thousand nine hundred and ninety nine
  (l) eight thousand and fifty four
4 (a) tens
  (b) thousands
  (c) hundreds
  (d) units
5 (a) largest 9731, smallest 1379
  (b) Pupil's answers
6 (a) 440   (b) 650   (c) 324
  (d) 2791   (e) 9160   (f) 5400
7 Pupils' answers

Exercise 1.2

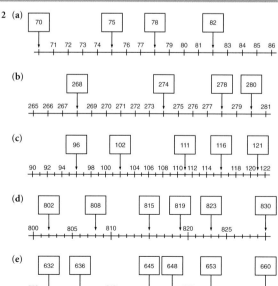

3 (a) 45   (b) 52   (c) 103   (d) 112
  (e) 129   (f) 137   (g) 256   (h) 262

4 (a) 9, 12, 32, 34, 66, 76
  (b) 17, 18, 26, 29, 30, 38
  (c) 38, 40, 45, 46, 47, 52
  (d) 87, 89, 95, 99, 103, 108
  (e) 109, 129, 130, 146, 162, 190
  (f) 109, 127, 148, 172, 174, 190
  (g) 704, 710, 718, 725, 762, 764
  (h) 930, 1055, 1422, 1529, 1627, 1657

5 Elliot, Gina, Callum, Alice, Denise, Fran, Ben

6 Mackenzie, Lena, Amur, Congo, Amazon, Nile

Exercise 1.3

1 (a)    56 is 60 to the nearest ten

  (b)    34 is 30 to the nearest ten

  (c)    99 is 100 to the nearest ten

  (d)    427 is 430 to the nearest ten

  (e)    612 is 610 to the nearest ten

  (f)    1008 is 1010 to the nearest ten

  (g)    75 is 70 or 80 to the nearest ten

  (h) 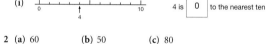   1476 is 1480 to the nearest ten

  (i)   4 is 0 to the nearest ten

2 (a) 60   (b) 50   (c) 80
  (d) 40   (e) 30   (f) 10
  (g) 20   (h) 70   (i) 30
  (j) 40   (k) 10   (l) 30
  (m) 50   (n) 100   (o) 0
3 (a) 150   (b) 240   (c) 150
  (d) 370   (e) 290   (f) 520
  (g) 580   (h) 300   (i) 700
  (j) 740   (k) 380   (l) 1000

4 Niagara 50, Angel 980, Jugela 950, Yosemite 740, Sutherland 580, Kjellfossen 560

6 (a) 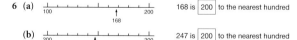   168 is 200 to the nearest hundred

  (b)   247 is 200 to the nearest hundred

  (c)   285 is 300 to the nearest hundred

  (d)   738 is 700 to the nearest hundred

  (e)   612 is 600 to the nearest hundred

  (f)   1235 is 1200 to the nearest hundred

  (g)   1875 is 1900 to the nearest hundred

7 (a) 273 → ☐300☐ (b) 141 → ☐100☐

(c) 472 → ☐500☐ (d) 314 → ☐300☐

(e) 586 → ☐600☐ (f) 921 → ☐900☐

(g) 687 → ☐700☐ (h) 299 → ☐300☐

(i) 147 → ☐100☐ (j) 385 → ☐400☐

(k) 560 → ☐600☐ (l) 1365 → ☐1400☐

Exercise 1.4

1 (a) 72 (b) 95 (c) 91 (d) 83 (e) 132
(f) 155 (g) 144 (h) 271 (i) 416 (j) 262
(k) 87 (l) 140 (m) 221 (n) 446 (o) 1315

2 (a) 69 (b) 51 (c) 41
(d) 82 (e) 140 (f) 159
(g) 218 (h) 231 (i) 292

3 £61
4 £51
5 Friday   27   Total   97 km
   Saturday 35
   Sunday   35
6 £292
7 (a) Yes (£16) (b) No (£17)
(c)

ITEM 1	ITEM 2	ITEM 3	TOTAL COST
hand cream	soap	body spray	12
shower gel	hand cream	body spray	16
bath oil	hand cream	soap	16
bath oil	soap	bbody spray	15
soap	body spray	perfume	16

Exercise 1.5

1 (a) 42 (b) 25 (c) 46 (d) 68 (e) 35
(f) 63 (g) 108 (h) 191 (i) 207 (j) 286
(k) 365 (l) 662 (m) 595 (n) 463 (o) 194

2 (a) 58 (b) 49 (c) 68 (d) 35 (e) 82
(f) 716 (g) 282 (h) 179 (i) 283

3 26
4 12°C
5 £361
6 86 cm
6 41

Exercise 1.6

1 (a) 18 (b) 32 (c) 15 (d) 36 (e) 56
(f) 45 (g) 81 (h) 30 (i) 24 (j) 28
(k) 39 (l) 48 (m) 88 (n) 135 (o) 192
(p) 192 (q) 392 (r) 203 (s) 240 (t) 200
(u) 324
(v)

number of people	2	3	5	9	11	14	15	18
number of sandwiches	4	6	10	18	22	28	30	36

(w)

number of people	1	3	4	8	12	15	16	18
number of bottles	3	9	12	24	36	45	48	54

2 (a) 21 (b) 15 (c) 24 (d) 21 (e) 48
(f) 36 (g) 72 (h) 42 (i) 32

3 (a) 60 (b) 70 (c) 161 (d) 496 (e) 176
(f) 21 (g) 111 (h) 513 (i) 747

4 £1.12
5 385 gms
6 144
7 285

Exercise 1.7

1 (a) 70 (b) 90 (c) 100 (d) 240
(e) 760 (f) 380 (g) 750 (h) 490
(i) 1250 (j) 1360 (k) 4820 (l) 2010

2 £60
3 £1.50
4 7650 kg
5 3240 g (3·24 kg)
6 1020

Exercise 1.8

1 (a)

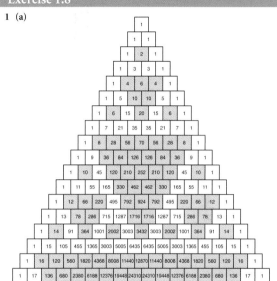

(b)

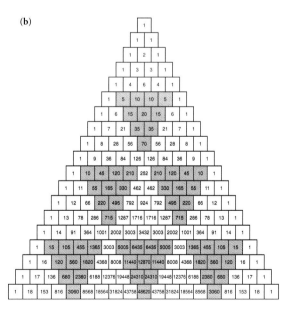

2 (a) 4 (b) 16 (c) 3 (d) 7 (e) 7
(f) 6 (g) 9 (h) 7 (i) 8

3 (a) 21 (b) 44 (c) 17 (d) 25 (e) 19 (f) 12
(g) 12 (h) 14 (i) 15 (j) 23 (k) 25 (l) 42

4 (a) 28 (b) 16 (c) 17 (d) 143 (e) 13
(f) 13 (g) 22 (h) 33 (i) 12

5 8 pencils
6 £20
7 7p
8 12 minutes

9 15 g
10 17
11 (a) 20   (b) 21   (c) 12
12

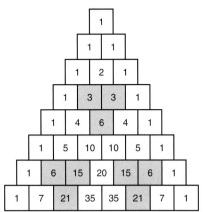

13

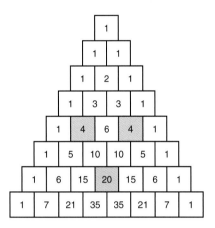

Exercise 1.9

1 (a) 16   (b) 82   (c) 54   (d) 26   (e) 47
   (f) 60   (g) 50   (h) 90   (i) 72
2 £45
3 35 strips
4 63 tables

Exercise 1.10

1 £537
2 165
3 157 cm
4 18
5 £520
6 £32
7 £31
8 (a) 15 kg   (b) 116 kg
   (c)

pupil 1	pupil 2	pupil 3	total wt (kg)
Claire	Nioma	Morven	35 + 40 + 44 = 119
Claire	Jed	Aisha	115
Claire	Jed	Gordon	117
Claire	Jed	Thomas	116
Claire	Jed	Leslie	115
Gordon	Nioma	Leslie	118
Jed	Aisha	Leslie	118
Claire	Jed	Leah	119
etc.			

Exercise 1.11

1 (a) 37   (b) 42   (c) 29   (d) 15   (e) 37
   (f) 23   (g) 62   (h) 51   (i) 46
2 (a) 21   (b) 32   (c) 23   (d) 22   (e) 322   (f) 243
   (g) 9   (h) 25   (i) 138   (j) 144   (k) 113   (l) 227
3 (a) 60   (b) 90   (c) 100   (d) 110   (e) 140   (f) 150
   (g) 200   (h) 220   (i) 210   (j) 110   (k) 90   (l) 140
   (m) 0   (n) 80   (o) 60   (p) 160   (q) 150   (r) 70
4 (a) 14   (b) 23   (c) 43   (d) 7   (e) 5   (f) 16
   (g) 13   (h) 8   (i) 9

Exercise 1.12

1

2 (a) 7, 8, 9, 10   (add 1)
   (b) 10, 12, 14, 16   (add 2)
   (c) 15, 18, 21, 24   (add 3)
   (d) 21, 25, 29, 33   (add 4)
   (e) 60, 70, 80, 90   (add 10)
   (f) 62, 72, 82, 92   (add 10)
   (g) 65, 75, 85, 95   (add 10)
   (h) 75, 78, 81, 84   (add 3)
   (i) 64, 59, 54, 49   (subtract 5)
   (j) 42, 36, 30, 24   (subtract 6)
3 (a) 35, 40   (b) 12, 14   (c) 26, 30
   (d) 8, 4   (e) 12, 6   (f) 8, 5
4 (a) 9, 11 add 2 to find the next number
   (b) 28, 34 add 6 to find the next number
   (c) 59, 71 add 12 to find the next number
   (d) 8, 0 subtract 8 to find the next number
   (e) 46, 55 add 9 to find the next number
   (f) 20, 0 subtract 20 to find the next number
5 (a) 213, 9, 11, 327, 17, 261, 1007
   (b) 68, 92, 914, 12, 104, 26, 638, 40, 8
6 (a) 5, 7, 9, 11, 13, 15, 17, 19, 21, 23
   (b) 7, 12, 17, 22, 27, 32, 37, 42, 47, 52
7 27 cm

Exercise 1.13

1 (a) 5   (b) −   (c) 6   (d) 5   (e) 6
   (f) 8   (g) 3   (h) ×   (i) 5   (j) 7
   (k) ÷   (l) 4   (m) 4   (n) −
2 (a) + 20   (b) − 4
     × 5   ÷ 3
3

Review exercise 1

1 (a) 280   (b) 604   (c) 4106   (d) 8050
2 (a) 32, 36, 49, 51, 58, 60
   (b) 208, 245, 268, 270, 271, 290
   (c) 1280, 1309, 1335, 1356, 1411, 1450
3 (a) 50   (b) 80   (c) 50   (d) 150
   (e) 130   (f) 210   (g) 170   (h) 200
4 241
5 48
6 14 p
7 £152
8 (a) 16, 19 add 3 to find the next number
   (b) 25, 30 add 5 to find the next number
   (c) 7, 5 subtract 2 to find the next number
   (d) 68, 72 add 4 to find the next number

Chapter 2

Exercise 2.1

1
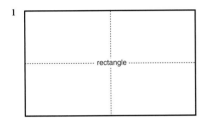

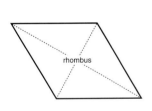
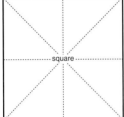
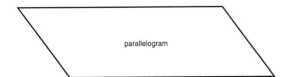

2 (a)   (b)   (c)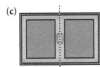

   (d)   (e)   (f) none

   (g)   (h) none (i)

(j) none   (k)   (l) none

(m) none   (n)   (o)

3 (a)   (b)   (c)

   (d)   (e)   (f)

   (g) none (h)   (i)

   (j) none (k)   (l) none

   (m)   (n)   (o)

4 (a) 1   (b) 2   (c) 0   (d) 4

5 (a)   (b)

   (c)   (d)

   (e)   (f)

Exercise 2.2

1 to **12** symmetrical: 1, 3, 5, 7, 8, 9, 10, 11

13 (**a**) Yes   (**b**) No   (**c**) Yes   (**d**) Yes

Exercise 2.3

1 (**a**)   (**b**)   (**c**)

2 (**a**) 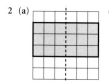   (**b**)   (**c**)

(**d**)   (**e**)   (**f**)

(**g**)   (**h**)   (**i**)

3 (**a**)   (**b**)   (**c**)

(**d**)   (**e**)   (**f**)

(**g**)   (**h**)   (**i**)

(**j**)   (**k**)   (**l**)

4 (**a**) 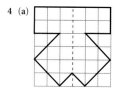   (**b**)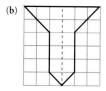

(**c**) 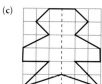   (**d**)

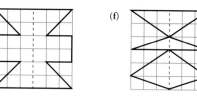

(**e**) 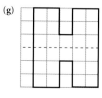   (**f**)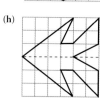

(**g**)   (**h**)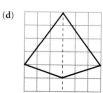

(**i**)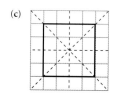

Review exercise 2

1 (**a**) Yes   (**b**) Yes   (**c**) Yes   (**d**) Yes   (**e**) No
2 (**a**) 4   (**b**) 0   (**c**) 1   (**d**) 0   (**e**) 1

3 (**a**) 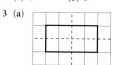   (**b**)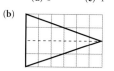

(**c**)    (**d**)

(**e**) 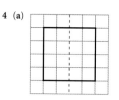   (**f**)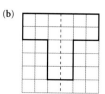

4 (**a**) 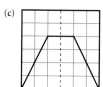   (**b**)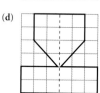

(**c**)   (**d**)

(e) 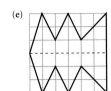   (f)

Chapter 3

Exercise 3.1

1 $\frac{1}{2}$ **2** $\frac{1}{3}$ **3** $\frac{1}{8}$

4 $\frac{1}{6}$ **5** $\frac{1}{5}$ **6** $\frac{1}{7}$

7 $\frac{1}{9}$ **8** $\frac{1}{10}$ **9** $\frac{1}{15}$

10 $\frac{1}{20}$ **11** $\frac{1}{12}$ **12** $\frac{1}{16}$

13 (a) 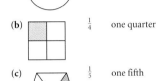 $\frac{1}{3}$ one third

(b) $\frac{1}{4}$ one quarter

(c) 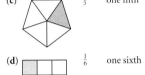 $\frac{1}{5}$ one fifth

(d) $\frac{1}{6}$ one sixth

(e) 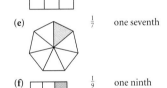 $\frac{1}{7}$ one seventh

(f) 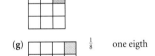 $\frac{1}{9}$ one ninth

(g) $\frac{1}{8}$ one eigth

14 (a) 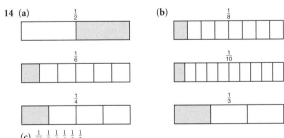   (b)

(c) $\frac{1}{10}, \frac{1}{8}, \frac{1}{6}, \frac{1}{4}, \frac{1}{3}, \frac{1}{2}$

Exercise 3.2

1 (a) $\frac{1}{3}$ (b) $\frac{2}{5}$ (c) $\frac{1}{6}$

(d) $\frac{3}{4}$ (e) $\frac{4}{9}$ (f) $\frac{3}{8}$

(g) $\frac{2}{7}$ (h) $\frac{3}{10}$ (i) $\frac{1}{9}$

(j) $\frac{5}{8}$ (k) $\frac{7}{10}$ (l) $\frac{3}{7}$

2 (a) $\frac{2}{3}$ (b) $\frac{5}{8}$ (c) $\frac{1}{6}$

(d) $\frac{5}{9}$ (e) $\frac{5}{12}$ (f) $\frac{2}{9}$

3 (a) $\frac{1}{3}$ (b) $\frac{3}{8}$ (c) $\frac{5}{6}$

(d) $\frac{4}{9}$ (e) $\frac{1}{12}$ (f) $\frac{2}{9}$

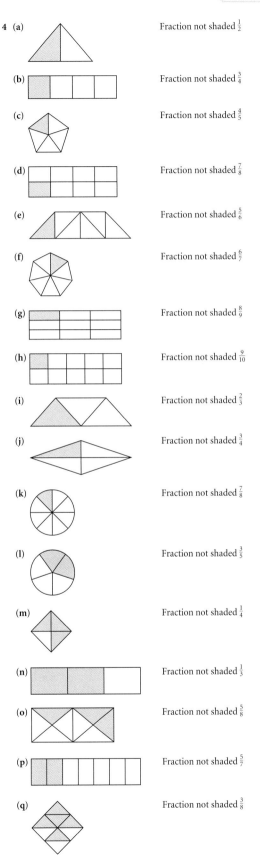

4 (a) Fraction not shaded $\frac{1}{2}$

(b) Fraction not shaded $\frac{3}{4}$

(c) Fraction not shaded $\frac{4}{5}$

(d) Fraction not shaded $\frac{7}{8}$

(e) Fraction not shaded $\frac{5}{6}$

(f) Fraction not shaded $\frac{6}{7}$

(g) Fraction not shaded $\frac{8}{9}$

(h) Fraction not shaded $\frac{9}{10}$

(i) Fraction not shaded $\frac{2}{3}$

(j) Fraction not shaded $\frac{3}{4}$

(k) Fraction not shaded $\frac{7}{8}$

(l) Fraction not shaded $\frac{3}{5}$

(m) Fraction not shaded $\frac{1}{4}$

(n) Fraction not shaded $\frac{1}{3}$

(o) Fraction not shaded $\frac{5}{8}$

(p) Fraction not shaded $\frac{5}{7}$

(q) Fraction not shaded $\frac{3}{8}$

(r) Fraction not shaded $\frac{1}{5}$

(s)

Fraction not shaded $\frac{5}{9}$

(t)

Fraction not shaded $\frac{1}{2}$

(u)

Fraction not shaded $\frac{5}{6}$

(v)

Fraction not shaded $\frac{3}{4}$

(w)

Fraction not shaded $\frac{1}{6}$

5 (a) (i) $\frac{1}{4}$ **(ii)** $\frac{3}{4}$ **(b) (i)** $\frac{3}{5}$ **(ii)** $\frac{2}{5}$
(c) (i) $\frac{3}{7}$ **(ii)** $\frac{4}{7}$ **(d) (i)** $\frac{4}{9}$ **(ii)** $\frac{5}{9}$
(e) (i) $\frac{4}{11}$ **(ii)** $\frac{7}{11}$ **(f) (i)** $\frac{5}{6}$ **(ii)** $\frac{1}{6}$
(g) (i) $\frac{3}{8}$ **(ii)** $\frac{5}{8}$ **(h) (i)** $\frac{1}{17}$ **(ii)** $\frac{16}{17}$
(i) (i) $\frac{6}{7}$ **(ii)** $\frac{1}{7}$

6 (a) (i) $\frac{1}{11}$ **(ii)** $\frac{4}{11}$ **(iii)** $\frac{6}{11}$

7 (a) $\frac{1}{25}$ **(b)** $\frac{8}{25}$ **(c)** $\frac{4}{25}$ **(d)** $\frac{12}{15}$

8 (a) $\frac{29}{90}$ **(b)** $\frac{43}{90}$ **(c)** $\frac{7}{90}$ **(d)** $\frac{11}{90}$

9 (i) $\frac{2}{7}$ **(ii)** $\frac{3}{7}$ **(iii)** $\frac{1}{7}$ **(iv)** $\frac{1}{7}$ **(v)** $\frac{2}{7}$

10 (a) $\frac{1}{6}, \frac{1}{8}$ **(b)** $\frac{1}{6}$ is bigger

11 (a) $\frac{1}{7}, \frac{1}{9}$ **(b)** $\frac{1}{7}$ is bigger

12 $\frac{1}{2}$ a pizza

13 $\frac{1}{4}$

14 $\frac{1}{6}, \frac{1}{5}, \frac{1}{4}, \frac{1}{3}, \frac{1}{2}$

Exercise 3.3

1 (a) 2 bananas **(b)** 3 apples **(c)** 5 cakes
(d) 6 sweets **(e)** 7 eggs **(f)** 10 mints
2 (a) £9 **(b)** 8 kg **(c)** 12 m **(d)** 15 km
(e) 20p **(f)** 50 miles **(g)** 22 g **(h)** £18
(i) £3.15 **(j)** 29 ℓ **(k)** 70 mm **(l)** 125 g
3 (a) 13 g **(b)** £42 **(c)** 28 kg **(d)** 36 m
(e) 72 cm **(f)** 250 ℓ **(g)** £224 **(h)** 63 ml
(i) 321 miles **(j)** 229 mm **(k)** £352 **(l)** 368 km
4 140 ml
5 £1.81
6 180 pupils

Exercise 3.4

1 (a) 2 miles **(b)** 1 cm **(c)** 3 km **(d)** 4 mm
(e) 7 kg **(f)** 5 ℓ **(g)** 6 mℓ **(h)** 10 g
2 (a) 1 km **(b)** 3 m **(c)** 4 mm **(d)** 5 cm
(e) 7 ℓ **(f)** 10 mℓ **(g)** 8 kg **(h)** 9 g
3 (a) £4 **(b)** 15 kg **(c)** 17 g
(d) 8 cm **(e)** £20 **(f)** 5 km
(g) £20 **(h)** 5 m **(i)** 9 ℓ
(j) 10 tonnes **(k)** 6 mm **(l)** 40°
4 (a) 5 **(b)** 12 **(c)** 6 **(d)** 5
(e) 7 **(f)** 8 **(g)** 7 **(h)** 4
(i) 6 **(j)** 8 **(k)** 9 **(l)** 9

5 (a)

Child	Bob	Ben	Mary
Fraction of £48	$\frac{1}{2}$	$\frac{1}{3}$	$\frac{1}{6}$
Amount received	£24	£16	£8

(b)

Item bought	meat	fish	vegetables	birthday present
Fraction of £56	$\frac{1}{8}$	$\frac{1}{7}$	$\frac{1}{4}$	the rest
Amount spent	£7	£8	£14	£27

(c)

Group	are girls	have fair hair	wear glasses	go home for lunch	have own computer	travel by bike
Fraction	$\frac{1}{2}$	$\frac{1}{3}$	$\frac{1}{4}$	$\frac{1}{5}$	$\frac{1}{9}$	$\frac{1}{10}$
Number in group	90	60	45	36	20	18

(d)

Colour	red	blue	green	white
Fraction of £48	$\frac{1}{3}$	$\frac{1}{5}$	$\frac{1}{10}$	the rest
Amount received	20	12	6	22

Review exercise 3

1 (a) $\frac{1}{4}$ **(b)** $\frac{1}{7}$ **(c)** $\frac{1}{12}$
2 (a) $\frac{4}{9}$ **(b)** $\frac{3}{7}$ **(c)** $\frac{7}{16}$
3 (a) $\frac{3}{11}$ **(b)** $\frac{6}{11}$ **(c)** $\frac{1}{11}$ **(d)** $\frac{5}{11}$
4 $\frac{1}{10}, \frac{1}{8}, \frac{1}{4}, \frac{1}{3}, \frac{1}{2}$
5 (a) £24 **(b)** 16 kg **(c)** £2.50 **(d)** 250 ml
6 (a) £9 **(b)** 6 tonnes **(c)** 3 g **(d)** 7 ℓ
7 (a) 9 **(b)** 12 **(c)** 6 **(d)** 9

Chapter 4

Exercise 4.1

1 (a) South stand **(b)** East stand **(c)** North stand

2
Building	Turn	Angle
Bank	$\frac{1}{4}$ turn clockwise	1 right angle
Church	$\frac{1}{4}$ turn anti-clockwise	1 right angle
Town Hall	$\frac{1}{2}$ turn	2 right angles
Cinema	Complete turn	4 right angles

3
Building	Turn	Angle
Tower	$\frac{1}{4}$ turn clockwise	2 right angles
Garden	$\frac{1}{4}$ turn anti-clockwise	1 right angle
Great Hall	$\frac{1}{2}$ turn	4 right angles
Gateway	Complete turn	1 right angle

4
Starting	Turn	Angle	Finishing Direction
North	$\frac{1}{2}$ turn	2 right angles	South
South	$\frac{1}{4}$ anti-clockwise	1 right angle	East
East	$\frac{1}{2}$ turn	2 right angles	West
West	$\frac{1}{4}$ cclockwise	1 right angle	North

5 (a)

quarter turn clockwise

half turn

full turn

(b)

quarter turn clockwise

half turn

full turn

6

From	To	Direction	Angle
1	2	clockwise	1 right angle
		anti-clockwise	3 right angles
1	3	clockwise	2 right angles
		anti-clockwise	2 right angles
1	4	anti-clockwise	1 right angle
		clockwise	3 right angles
2	1	anti-clockwise	1 right angle
		clockwise	3 right angles
4	1	clockwise	1 right angle
		anti-clockwise	3 right angles
4	2	clockwise	2 right angles
		anti-clockwise	2 right angles
3	1	clockwise	2 right angles
		anti-clockwise	2 right angles
3	4	clockwise	1 right angle
		anti-clockwise	3 right angles
2	3	clockwise	1 right angle
		anti-clockwise	3 right angles
4	3	anti-clockwise	1 right angle
		clockwise	3 right angles
3	2	anti-clockwise	1 right angle
		clockwise	3 right angles

7 (a) $\frac{1}{4}$ turn clockwise, 1 right angle

(b) $\frac{1}{2}$ turn clockwise or anti-clockwise, 2 right angles

(c) $\frac{1}{4}$ turn anti-clockwise, 1 right angle

Exercise 4.2

1 (a) ∠ABC   (b) ∠XTZ   (c) ∠DFE
(d) ∠VST   (e) ∠LMN   (f) ∠SAD

2 (a) (i) ∠BAD (ii) ∠DCB (iii) ∠ABC (iv) ∠ADC
(b) (i) ∠HEF (ii) ∠FGH (iii) ∠EFG (iv) ∠EHG

3

Exercise 4.3

2

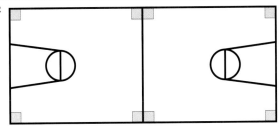

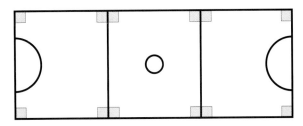

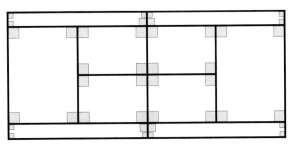

3 Pupils make list

4 (a) 3 o'clock and 9 o'clock   (b) 6 o'clock

5 (a) ∠ACE, ∠DCB   (b) ∠QOS, ∠ROT

6 Pupils make list

Exercise 4.4

1 (a) a, c, e, f   (b) b, d, g, h

2 (a) red   (b) blue   (c) yellow   (d) green

3 (a) ∠ABC acute   (b) ∠DEF obtuse
(c) ∠XZY acute   (d) ∠TSV obtuse

Exercise 4.5

1 (a) 60°   (b) 30°   (c) 80°   (d) 110°

2 (a) 20°   (b) 50°   (c) 70°   (d) 160°
(e) 110°   (f) 45°   (g) 135°   (h) 90°

3 (a) 90°   (b) 180°

Exercise 4.6

1 (a)   (b)   (c)   (d)   (e)   (f)   (g)   (h)

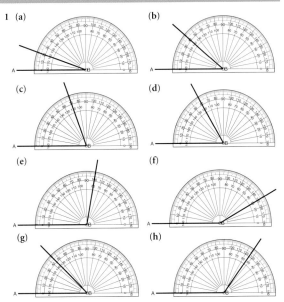

2 3 Pupils draw angles

Exercise 4.7

1 (a)

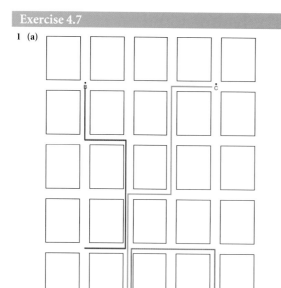

2 (a) Walk 2 blocks North.
Turn right 90°.
Walk 2 blocks.
Turn right 90°.
Walk 1 block.
Turn right 90°.
Walk 1 block.
Turn right 90°.
Walk 2 blocks.
Turn left 90°.
Walk 1 block.
Turn left 90°.
Walk 3 blocks.

(b) Walk 1 block North.
Turn left 90°.
Walk 2 blocks.
Turn right 90°.
Walk 1 block.
Turn right 90°.
Walk 3 blocks.
Turn right 90°.
Walk 1 block.
Turn right 90°.
Walk 1 block.
Turn left 90°.
Walk 1 block.

Review exercise 4

1 (a) South Stand   (b) East Stand   (c) North Stand
2 (a) ∠AWX   (b) ∠RTS   (c) ∠DEF
3

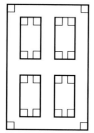

4 (a)

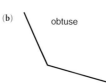

acute   (b) obtuse

(c)

right   (d)

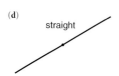

straight

5 (a) 40°   (b) 125°
6 Pupils draw angles
7 Walk 2 blocks North.
Turn right 90°.
Walk 1 block.
Turn right 90°.
Wlak 1 block.
Turn left 90°.
Walk 1 block.
Turn left 90°.
Walk 1 block.
Turn right 90°.
Walk 2 blocks.
Turn right 90°.
Walk 1 block.
Turn right 90°.
Walk 1 block.
Turn left 90°.
Walk 1 block.
Turn right 90°.
Walk 2 blocks.

Chapter 5

Exercise 5.1

1 (a) £2.16 (b) £1.65 (c) £4.12 (d) £3.72
(e) £0.85 (f) £0.48 (g) £0.10 (h) £0.02
2 (a) 100 p (b) 200 p (c) 400 p (d) 350 p (e) 202 p
(f) 222 p (g) 105 p (h) 164 p (i) 675 p
3 (a) £1.65 (b) £8.99 (c) £2.20 (d) £0.99
(e) £0.50 (f) £0.05
4 (a) £3.25 (b) £6.19 (c) £9.03 (d) £0.78
(e) £5.30 (f) £0.98 (g) £0.20 (h) £0.06
(i) £0.50 (j) £0.02 (k) £14.10 (l) £10.20
5 (a) 723 p (b) 925 p (c) 480 p (d) 106 p
(e) 75 p (f) 80 p (g) 9 p (h) 1002 p

Exercise 5.2

1 (a) £5.39 (b) £5.90 (c) £2.31 (d) £5.11
(e) £4.28 (f) £11.06 (g) £17.31 (h) £25.40
(i) £32.60 (j) £30.02 (k) £21.66 (l) £31.10
2 (a) £3.95 (b) £7.13 (c) £8.32
(d) £7.99 (e) £14.01 (f) £18.73
3 (a) £6.30 (b) £8.32
4 (a) £20.43 (b) £20.10 (c) £31.90
5 (a) £7.97 (b) £1.93 (c) £8.70
(d) £7.99 (e) £14.01 (f) £17.73
6 (a) £10.10 (b) £10.34 (c) £29.01
7 (a) £3.97 (b) £17.49 (c) £42.54
8 (a) £4.79 (b) £7.88 (c) £6.02 (d) £20.11
9 (a) £11.75 (b) £13.99 (c) £4.27
10 (a) £27.84 (b) £37.42

Exercise 5.3

1 (a) £3.11 (b) £2.60 (c) £3.11 (d) £1.29
(e) £2.90 (f) £4.83 (g) £10.83 (h) £8.82
(i) £0.99 (j) £0.86 (k) £19.07 (l) £1.12
2 (a) £2.33 (b) £0.09 (c) £2.84
(d) £2.96 (e) £4.97 (f) £17.89
3 (a) 19 p (b) £4.19
4 (a) £10.87 (b) £6.02 (c) £8.99
5 (a) £2.44 (b) £4.44 (c) £2.40
(d) £3.24 (e) £1.87 (f) £3.21
(g) £5.96 (h) £4.91 (i) £5.78
6 (a) 55 p (b) 21 p (c) 16 p
7 (a) £1.35 (b) £2.57 (c) £3.12
8 (a) £6.35 (b) 41 p (c) £2.32
9 (a) £2.80 (b) 55 p (c) £3.87
10 (a) £11.65 (b) £22.19
11 £3.64

Exercise 5.4

1 (a) 6·15   (b) 9·41   (c) 5·89
   (d) 1·06   (e) 0·73   (f) 0·9
   (g) 0·01   (h) 10·1   (i) 0·2
2 (a) £3.62   (b) £1.15   (c) £6.41   (d) £0.97
   (e) £0.03   (f) £3.10   (g) £14.50   (h) £0.80
3 (a) £20.13   (b) £15.10   (c) £20.08
   (d) £18.70   (e) £86.60   (f) £110.80
4 (a) £4.35   (b) £1.51   (c) £4.11
   (d) £2.75   (e) £14.40   (f) £53.54
5 (a) £12.07   (b) £16.04   (c) £19.90   (d) £12.80
   (e) £96.10   (f) £66.90   (g) £58.60   (h) £17.87
6 (a) £4.21   (b) £3.38   (c) £1.25
   (d) £0.39   (e) £2.70   (f) £2.30
7 (a) £8.90   (b) £8.30   (c) £11.00   (d) £32.20
   (e) £0.30   (f) £14.50   (g) £120   (h) £125
8 (a) £1.09   (b) £1.20   (c) £0.90   (d) £4.10
   (e) £0.80   (f) £0.70   (g) £4.08   (h) £0.80
9 £6.15
10 £1.25
11 £13
12 £2.90
13 Yes; 40 p left
14 £17
15 £0.70
16 £2.40
17 £2.40
18 £31.10

Revision exercise 5

1 (a) £2.25   (b) £0.90
2 (a) £3.56   (b) £8.60   (c) £0.67   (d) £0.02
3 (a) 575p   (b) 180p   (c) 305p   (d) 10p
4 (a) £3.79   (b) £3.80   (c) £6.31   (d) £7.05   (e) £9.91
   (f) £19.22   (g) £2.24   (h) £3.14   (i) £0.73
5 (a) £5.96   (b) £3.59   (c) £0.68
   (d) £5.96   (e) £6.93   (f) £14.11
6 75p
7 (a) £2.91   (b) £3.01   (c) £0.40
8 (a) £6.20   (b) £0.80   (c) £0.40
9 £3.60

Chapter 6

Exercise 6.1

1 (a) mackerel, flounder, snapper, shark
2 (a) Sid, Tim, Ned, Ben
3 (a) birch, oak, beech, pine
4 (a) 3 cm approx.   (b) 8 cm approx.
   (c) 12 cm approx.   (d) 4·5 cm approx.
5 (a) Your answer   (b) Lines are the same length.

Exercise 6.2

1 (a) 2 cm   (b) 5 cm   (c) 3 cm   (d) 8 cm   (e) 6 cm
3 (a) 7 cm   (b) 6 cm   (c) 4 cm
   (d) 10 cm   (e) 9 cm   (f) 5 cm
4 10 cm
5–11 Pupil's own answers

Exercise 6.3

1 (a) 3 m   (b) 6 m   (c) 5 m   (d) 9 m
   (e) 11 m   (f) 19 m   (g) 20 m   (h) 25 m
   (i) 3 m 25 cm   (j) 4 m 85 cm   (k) 5 m 50 cm   (l) 0·5 m or 50 cm
2 (a) 400 cm   (b) 700 cm   (c) 800 cm   (d) 1200 cm
   (e) 850 cm   (f) 625 cm   (g) 275 cm   (h) 315 cm
   (i) 2500 cm   (j) 3300 cm   (k) 4200 cm   (l) 5500 cm
3, 4, 5 Pupil's own answers

6 (a) Cal, Alex, Bob, Tom
   (b) 2 m 10 cm, 1 m 90 cm, 1 m 80 cm, 1 m 65 cm
7 (a) yellow, blue, green, red
   (b) 2 m 40 cm, 2 m 20 cm, 1 m 95 cm, 1 m 90 cm
8 (a) 2 m, 5 m, 7 m, 8 m
   (b) 3 cm, 18 cm, 25 cm, 75 cm
   (c) 3 m 99 cm, 5 m 19 cm, 5 m 25 cm, 6 m 2 cm,
   (d) 1 m 99 cm, 2 m 95 cm, 3 m 9 cm, 8 m 1 cm,

Exercise 6.4

1 hummingbird, magpie, parrot, eagle, swan
2 (a) 54 kg   (b) 62 kg   (c) 58·5 kg
   (d) 65·25 kg   (e) 72·75 kg   (f) 50·75 kg
4 (a) 4 kg   (b) 6 kg   (c) 9 kg
   (d) 7 kg   (e) 4 kg 500 g   (f) 7 kg 500 g
   (g) 5 kg 500 g   (h) 1 kg 500 g   (i) 2 kg 300 g
   (j) 3 kg 600 g   (k) 8 kg 900 g   (l) 4 kg 200 g
5 (a) 4000 g   (b) 6000 g   (c) 9000 g   (d) 7000 g
   (e) 5500 g   (f) 3400 g   (g) 8200 g   (h) 4200 g
   (i) 2700 g   (f) 6900 g   (g) 7300 g   (h) 8700 g

Exercise 6.5

1 (a) 1ℓ   (b) $\frac{1}{2}$ℓ   (c) $\frac{1}{4}$ℓ   (d) $\frac{3}{4}$ℓ
2 (a) 2   (e) 500 millilitres = $\frac{1}{2}$ litre
3 (d) 4   (e) 250 millilitres = $\frac{1}{4}$ litre
4 1000

Review exercise 6

1 (a) 3 cm   (b) 7 cm
3 (a) 4 m   (b) 8 m   (c) 4 m 50 cm   (d) 6 m 20 cm
4 (a) 500 cm   (b) 900 cm   (c) 250 cm   (d) 325 cm
5 (a) 3 m, 4 m, 6 m, 9 m,
   (b) 22 cm, 23 cm, 25 cm, 26 cm,
   (c) 99 cm, 3 m 8 cm, 3 m 15 cm, 7 m 15 cm
6 (a) 5 kg   (b) 8 kg   (c) 6 kg 500 g   (d) 8 kg 200 g
7 (a) 2000 g   (b) 3000 g   (c) 7500 g   (d) 9300 g
8 (a) 2 ℓ   (b) 1$\frac{1}{2}$ ℓ

Chapter 7

Exercise 7.1

1 (a) 100 mm   (b) 120 mm   (c) 110 mm   (d) 160 cm
   (e) 180 cm   (f) 60 cm   (g) 106 cm   (h) 37 cm
2 (a) 28 cm   (b) 58 mm   (c) 20 cm   (d) 40 cm
   (e) 10 cm   (f) 62 mm   (g) 48 cm   (h) 30 cm
   (i) 50 mm   (j) 48 cm   (k) 51 mm   (l) 37 cm
   (m) 29 mm   (n) 36 cm   (o) 60 mm   (p) 41 cm
   (q) 30 cm
3 (a) 12 cm   (b) 12 cm
4 (a) 14 cm   (b) 10 cm   (c) 12 cm
   (d) 16 cm   (e) 14 cm   (f) 14 cm
5 (a) 15 cm   (b) 12 cm   (c) 14 cm
   (d) 14 cm   (e) 14 cm   (f) 12 cm
   (g) 16 cm   (h) 18 cm   (i) 10 cm

Exercise 7.2

1 (a) 6 cm^2 (b) 6 cm^2 (c) 7 cm^2
   (d) 6 cm^2 (e) 9 cm^2 (f) 8 cm^2
2 (a) 9 cm^2 (b) 12 cm^2 (c) 16 cm^2
   (d) 15 cm^2 (e) 20 cm^2
3 (a) 8 cm^2 (b) 11 cm^2 (c) 8 cm^2
   (d) 7 cm^2 (e) 8 cm^2 (f) 13 cm^2
4 (a) 7·5 cm^2 (b) 11 cm^2 (c) 10 cm^2
   (d) 4 cm^2 (e) 8 cm^2 (f) 8 cm^2
   (g) 12 cm^2 (h) 16 cm^2 (i) 13 cm^2
   (j) 10 cm^2 (k) 7 cm^2 (l) 13$\frac{1}{2}$ cm^2

5 (a) Area = 8 cm²
      Perimeter = 16 cm
   (b) Area = 8 cm²
      Perimeter = 16 cm
   (c) Area = 8 cm²
      Perimeter = 18 cm
   (d) Area = 7 cm²
      Perimeter = 16 cm
   (e) Area = 12 cm²
      Perimeter = 18 cm
   (f) Area = 11 cm²
      Perimeter = 24 cm
6 (a) Area = 16 cm²
      Perimeter = 24 cm
   (b) Area = 10 cm²
      Perimeter = 19·8 cm
   (c) Area = 9 cm²
      Perimeter = 20 cm
   (d) Area = $8\frac{1}{2}$ cm²
      Perimeter = 14·2 cm
   (e) Area = 12 cm²
      Perimeter = 26 cm
   (f) Area = $14\frac{1}{2}$ cm²
      Perimeter = 23·2 cm

Exercise 7.3

1 (a) 8 cm²   (b) 9 cm²   (c) 5 cm²   (d) 12 cm²
   (e) 18 cm² (f) 16 cm² (g) 5 cm²

2 99 cm²

3 150 cm²

4 100 cm²

5 60 cm²

6 96 cm²

7 81 cm²

8 (a) P 160 cm², Q 16 cm², R 16 cm²
   (b) A 36 cm², B 36 cm², C 36 cm² D 36 cm²
   (c) No

Review exercise 7

1 (a) 110 mm   (b) 160 mm   (c) 90 mm   (d) 200 mm
   (e) 60 cm   (f) 72 cm   (g) 67 cm   (h) 52 cm
   (i) 57 cm   (j) 110 cm

2 (a) 7 cm²   (b) 9 cm²   (c) 11 cm²   (d) 11 cm²
   (e) 6 cm²   (f) 12 cm²   (g) 8 cm²   (h) 9 cm²

3 (a) 9 cm²   (b) 8 cm²   (c) $8\frac{1}{2}$ cm²

4 (a) 15 cm²   (b) 9 cm²   (c) 7 cm²

5 150 cm²

6 64 cm²

Chapter 8

Exercise 8.1

1 get up, get dressed, breakfast, go to school, morning break, lunch, school ends, get the bus home, tea, do homework, watch television.

2 read recipe, go to shops, buy ingredients, mix ingredients, pour into baking tin, turn oven on, put into oven, remove from oven, leave to cool, decorate cake, eat cake.

3 (a) morning   (b) morning
   (c) morning   (d) evening
   (e) morning   (f) afternoon
   (g) morning   (h) evening
   (i) evening   (j) evening

Exercise 8.2

1 (a) half past two   (b) seven o'clock
   (c) five past five   (d) quarter to one
   (e) twenty five to two (f) ten past nine
   (g) five to twelve   (h) quarter past four
   (i) ten to three   (j) twenty past six
   (k) ten past eight   (l) twenty to four
   (m) twenty five to eleven (n) twenty five past one
   (o) ten to one.

2

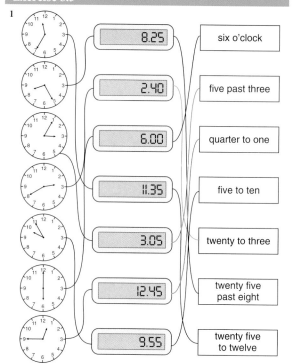

3 (a) half past five   (b) quarter past eleven
   (c) quarter to seven   (d) quarter past eight
   (e) half past four   (f) seven o'clock
   (g) twelve o'clock   (h) quarter to ten
   (i) quarter past one

4 (a) twenty five past eleven (b) ten past six
   (c) twenty five past three   (d) ten to three
   (e) five to nine   (f) twenty to eight
   (g) twenty past twelve   (h) five past three
   (i) twenty five to seven.

Exercise 8.3

1

2 (a) 3 : 25 (b) 10 : 15 (c) 8 : 05 (d) 4 : 50
 (e) 8 : 30 (f) 6 : 40 (g) 10 : 35 (h) 5 : 45
3 (a)

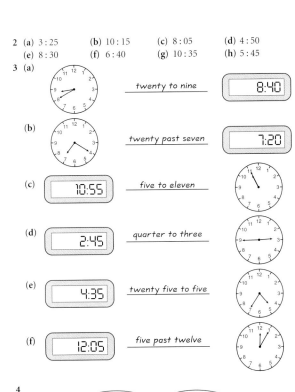

(b)
(c)
(d)
(e)
(f)

4

5 (a) yes (b) 10:15 (c) 4:30

Exercise 8.4

1 (a) 7.00 p.m. (b) 12.30 p.m. (c) 8.00 a.m.
 (d) 7.30 a.m. (e) 4.30 p.m. (f) 11.15 a.m.
2 (a) 6.15 a.m. (b) 3.30 p.m. (c) 6.40 p.m. (d) 12.25 p.m.
 (e) 8.50 a.m. (f) 6.10 p.m. (g) 8.15 a.m. (h) 6.35 a.m.
 (i) 4.50 p.m.

Exercise 8.5

1 4 hours 2 20 mins 3 55 mins 4 35 mins
5 7.40 p.m. 6 8.00 p.m. 7 7.50 a.m.
8 (a) 6.55 p.m. (b) 10.55 p.m. (c) 30 mins (d) 45 mins
 (e) Lord of the Wings (f) 1 hr 45 mins
9 (a) 3.42 (b) 3.55 (c) 13 mins (d) 45 mins

Exercise 8.6

1 2 hrs 2 6 hours 3 6 hrs 30 mins 4 2 p.m.
5 (a) 11.33, 11.53, 12.40
 (b) 28 mins (c) 12.38 (d) 45 mins

Exercise 8.7

1 January, February, March, April, May, June, July, August, September, October, November, December
2 (a) 31 (b) 30 (c) 30 (d) 31 (e) 31 (f) 31
3 (a) Jan, Feb (b) Jan, Feb, Mar, Apr, May, Jun
4 (a) Dec (b) Sep, Oct, Nov, Dec
5 (a) True (b) True (c) True
 (d) False (e) False (f) False
6 (a) 6th of July 2004
 (b) 25th of November 2003
 (c) 28th of February 2003
7 (a) 4/4/02 (b) 10/8/04 (c) 21/12/04 (d) 12/1/05
8 (a) 7th (b) 16th (c) Friday (d) Thursday (e) 25th
9 (a) 5 (b) Sunday (c) Saturday (d) 1, 8, 15, 22, 29 (e) 3rd December (f) 2nd December
 (g) 30th October (h) 26th August
10 (a) 36 (b) 48 (c) 72
11 (a) 104 (b) 156 (c) 208

Review exercise 8

1 (a) half past eight (b) quarter past two
 (c) quarter to four (d) twenty five to eight
 (e) ten to twelve (f) five past eight
2 (a) 8 : 25 (b) 2 : 15 (c) 11 : 45 (d) 8 : 50
3 (a) 3.30 p.m. (b) 10.50 a.m. (c) 7.20 p.m. (d) 12.35 p.m.
4 (a) $4\frac{1}{2}$ hours 4 h 30 mins
5 (a) $3\frac{1}{4}$ hours 3 h 15 mins
6 (a) 30 (b) 31 (c) 31 (d) 31
7 (a) 22nd April 2004
 (b) 15th August 2004
 (c) 17th October 2003
8 24
9 (a) 5th (b) 4 (c) Monday
 (c) 24th (d) 17th (e) 5

Chapter 9

Exercise 9.1

1 (a) £8.30 (b) £7.50 (c) £6.80
 (d) £5.20 (e) £10.00 (f) £12.00
2 (a) £6.80 (b) £12.00
 £8.30 £7.50
 £5.20 £7.50
 —————— ——————
 £20.30 £27.00

3 (a) Football (b) 30 min (c) Talent show
 (d) 6.00 p.m. (e) 2.20 p.m. (f) 10.00 am
 (g) 1 hr 30 min (h) Swimming
4 (a) £3 (b) £3.50 (c) £3.50 (d) £5
 (e) £22 (f) 14
5 (a) 11.00 am (b) 6.00 p.m. (c) 6.45 p.m. (d) 45 mins
6 (a) 15 (b) 12 (c) Fleming (d) Burns
 (e) 15 (f) Wallace
7 (a) 20 (b) 8 (c) 5 (d) 12
 (e) 12 (f) 8
8 (a) 16 (b) 10 (c) 2 (d) 12
 (e) 0 (f) 8

Exercise 9.2

1
Scones	Doughnuts	Pastries	Buns
6	12	4	8

2
Small spoons	Forks	Knives	Large spoons
6	5	3	2

3

Tomato	Pea	Lentil	Broth	Carrot
4	1	1	2	3

4

	Black	White	Spotty	Striped
Small	2	1	5	1
Large	1	0	4	2

5

	36	37	38	39
Rebos	3	2	1	3
Adilas	4	5	2	3

6

	36	37	38	39
Rebos	2	5	0	1
Adilas	5	4	2	3

7

	Maths	English
Kylie	76	61
Jason	92	58
Charlene	61	60
Scott	43	58

8

	French	Science
John	61	45
Paul	85	75
George	66	49
Ringo	35	52

9

Class	School dinners	Packed lunches
1B1	19	7
1B2	13	12
1F1	22	5
1F2	20	8

10

	French	German
1B1	3	9
1B2	7	12
1F1	0	18
2F2	15	15

Exercise 9.3

1 (a) 6   (b) 7   (c) 3   (d) 4   (e) 2   (f) 8
2 (a) Monday   (b) Tuesday and Friday
   (c) M Tu W Th F
       6   4   5   3   4
3 (a) 6   (b) 10 a.m.   (c) 12 noon   (d) 44
4 (a) 16   (b) 14   (c) Cream   (d) Walnut
5 (a) Sam   (b) £60   (c) £15   (d) Sarah   (e) £40
6 (a) 18   (b) August   (c) September   (d) June
7 (a) 70   (b) 2003   (c) 2004   (d) 10
8 (a) Friday   (b) Monday (c) 400   (d) Monday (e) 2700

Exercise 9.4

1 (a) bus   (b) cycle   (c) 9   (d) 4
2 (a) 10   (b) 9   (c) Science
3 (a) Jets   (b) Sharks   (c) 15   (d) 10
4 (a) Raffle   (b) Class collection   (c) £15
   (d) Sponsored walk   (e) £75
5 (a) 4 door   (b) 4 Wd   (c) 12   (d) 2 door   (e) 49
6 (a) 6 hrs   (b) Mhairi   (c) Tam   (d) Sue   (e) 28
7 (a) 2   (b) 2   (c) Thistle   (d) Rovers and City
8 (a) 2B1   (b) 2F1   (c) 2F1   (d) 2W1   (e) girls   (f) 155

Exercise 9.5

1

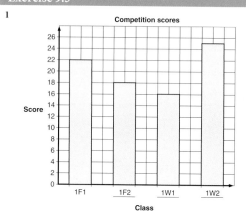

2

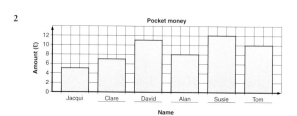

3

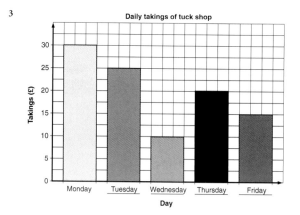

4

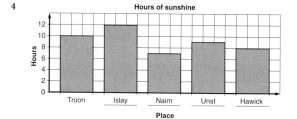

5

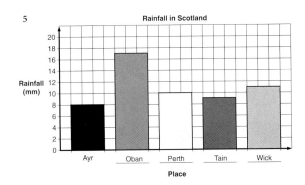

6

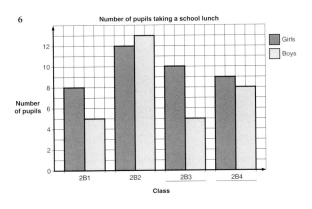

7

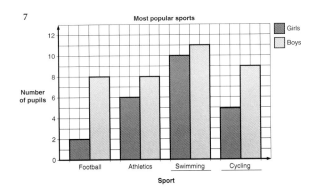

8

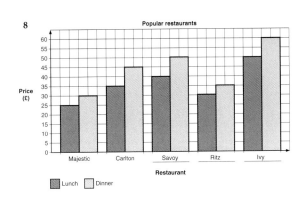

9

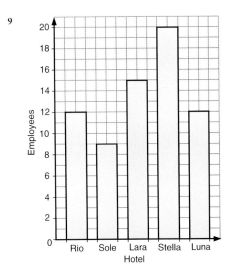

10

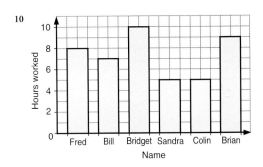

Review exercise 9

1 (a) £4.50   (b) 18   (c) £17
2 (a) £0.65   (b) £1   (c) Kola and Lift, 500 ml
   (d) £2

3

	Lavender	Rose	Magnolia
Large	2	1	3
Small	3	5	4

4 (a) 14   (b) Blueberry
   (c) Poppyseed   (d) Orange
5 (a) 10   (b) Swimming
   (c) Skating   (d) Cycling
6 (a) 12–1 p.m.   (b) 9–10 a.m.
   (c) 18   (d) 10–11 a.m.
7 (a) Friday   (b) Wednesday
   (c) Tuesday   (d) 12

8

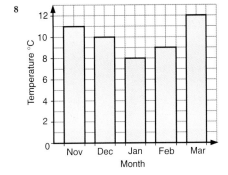

9

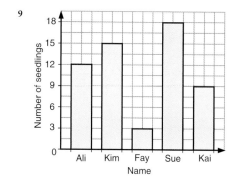

Chapter 10

Exercise 10.1

1 (a) $x + 3 = 9$ (b) $x + 3 = 9$ (c) $x + 3 = 9$
     $x = 6$ $x = 2$ $m = 1$
  (d) $q + 6 = 16$ (e) $3 + f = 6$ (f) $y + 1 = 23$
     $q = 10$ $f = 3$ $y = 22$

2 (a) $x = 7$ (b) $y = 3$ (c) $c = 2$
  (d) $z = 10$ (e) $x = 4$ (f) $y = 4$
  (g) $x = 15$ (h) $z = 7$ (i) $c = 6$
  (j) $x = 11$ (k) $y = 10$ (l) $z = 7$
  (m) $y = 30$ (n) $m = 20$ (o) $y = 6$
  (p) $z = 9$ (q) $x = 9$ (r) $x = 13$
  (s) $p = 17$ (t) $y = 5$ (u) $z = 9$
  (v) $r = 30$ (w) $z = 50$ (x) $y = 35$

3 (a) $y = 13$ (b) $x = 15$ (c) $c = 14$
  (d) $m = 11$ (e) $g = 22$ (f) $x = 7$
  (g) $x = 75$ (h) $y = 100$ (i) $j = 45$
  (j) $m = 28$ (k) $z = 16$ (l) $s = 60$
  (m) $x = 27$ (n) $y = 14$ (o) $x = 15$

Exercise 10.2

1 (a) $x - 4 = 3$ (b) $12 - y = 10$ (c) $6 - p = 5$
     $x = 7$ $y = 2$ $p = 1$
  (d) $a - 5 = 4$ (e) $m - 7 = 5$ (f) $8 - s = 2$
     $a = 9$ $m = 12$ $s = 6$

2 (a) $x = 8$ (b) $y = 15$ (c) $z = 5$ (d) $m = 10$
  (e) $z = 12$ (f) $y = 10$ (g) $x = 1$ (h) $y = 10$
  (i) $s = 10$ (j) $m = 20$ (k) $r = 50$ (l) $y = 16$
  (m) $y = 10$ (n) $x = 6$ (o) $x = 2$ (p) $r = 20$
  (q) $p = 1$ (r) $z = 5$ (s) $y = 15$ (t) $x = 20$
  (u) $a = 7$ (v) $z = 12$ (w) $f = 0$ (x) $x = 12$

Exercise 10.3

1 (a) $x = 13$ (b) $y = 8$ (c) $y = 1$ (d) $b = 3$ (e) $z = 4$
  (f) $m = 15$ (g) $x = 20$ (h) $m = 4$ (i) $x = 4$ (j) $y = 13$
  (k) $x = 30$ (l) $z = 20$ (m) $y = 10$ (n) $a = 7$ (o) $a = 16$
  (p) $m = 20$ (q) $y = 0$ (r) $f = 35$

2 (a) $y = 15$ (b) $x = 7$ (c) $z = 29$ (d) $p = 11$
  (e) $x = 12$ (f) $y = 20$ (g) $x = 100$ (h) $x = 15$
  (i) $y = 20$ (j) $y = 25$ (k) $x = 100$ (l) $x = 8$

Exercise 10.4

1 $x = 3$ 2 $x = 10$ 3 $x = 6$ 4 $x = 6$
5 $x = 8$ 6 $x = 10$ 7 $x = 8$ 8 $x = 9$
9 $x = 6$ 10 $x = 5$ 11 $x = 6$ 12 $x = 5$
13 $x = 4$ 14 $x = 6$

Exercise 10.5

1 (a) $4a = 12$ (b) $6c = 60$ (c) $5x = 25$
     $a = 3$ $c = 10$ $x = 5$

  (d) $4m = 8$ (e) $2f = 14$ (f) $3s = 9$
     $m = 2$ $f = 7$ $s = 3$

2 (a) $y = 2$ (b) $m = 4$ (c) $p = 5$ (d) $y = 3$ (e) $x = 5$
  (f) $x = 7$ (g) $p = 10$ (h) $y = 10$ (i) $z = 4$ (j) $x = 7$
  (k) $y = 7$ (l) $z = 30$ (m) $z = 7$ (n) $y = 6$ (o) $x = 1$
  (p) $y = 3$ (q) $y = 8$ (r) $y = 9$ (s) $z = 1$ (t) $z - 6$
  (u) $y = 50$ (v) $p = 3$ (w) $y = 10$ (x) $m = 0$

Review exercise 10

1 (a) $x = 6$ (b) $y = 9$ (c) $z = 9$ (d) $p = 7$ (e) $m = 12$
  (f) $y = 13$ (g) $x = 15$ (h) $z = 25$ (i) $y = 100$
2 (a) $y = 20$ (b) $x = 20$ (c) $m = 2$ (d) $y = 1$ (e) $x = 3$
  (f) $z = 30$ (g) $y = 14$ (h) $z = 50$ (i) $x = 100$
3 (a) $y = 6$ (b) $y = 6$ (c) $m = 8$ (d) $z = 9$ (e) $x = 9$
  (f) $m = 4$ (g) $x = 9$ (h) $y = 1$ (i) $x = 4$
4 (a) $y = 10$ (b) $x = 20$ (c) $z = 3$ (d) $m = 2$
  (e) $z = 11$ (f) $p = 8$ (g) $z = 7$ (h) $z = 30$
  (i) $x = 1$ (j) $y = 2$ (k) $x = 13$ (l) $y = 5$
5 (a) $y = 9$ (b) $y = 8$

Chapter 11

Exercise 11.1

1 A(3, 1)   B(1, 3)   C(5, 4)   D(1, 1)   E(3, 3)   F(4, 5)
  G(3, 0)   H(4, 2)   J(0, 2)   K(2, 1)   L(1, 2)   M(3, 5)
  N(1, 4)   P(4, 0)   Q(0, 3)   R(6, 4)   S(1, 5)   T(0, 0)
  U(6, 0)   V(8, 3)   W(9, 5)   Z(10, 2)

2 A(2, 5)   B(3, 4)   C(4, 0)   D(0, 1)   E(2, 3)   F(1, 5)
  G(4, 4)   H(5, 2)   J(4, 0)   K(0, 1)   L(1, 2)   M(6, 5)
  N(7, 2)   Q(0, 5)   P(5, 0)   R(8, 0)

3 Town (6, 3)   Village (3, 0)   Harbour (3, 10)
  Cave (6, 6)   Hideout (9, 8)   Lighthouse (11, 1)
  Rock (11, 10)   Pirate port (0, 7)   Mountain (3, 7)
  Shipwreck (1, 5)   Treasure (11, 5)

Exercise 11.2

1

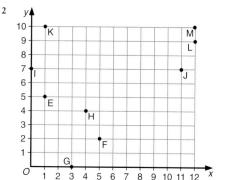

2

3

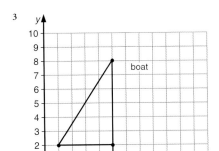

boat

7

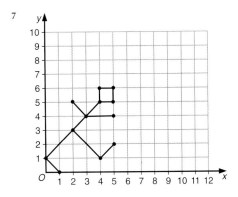

4

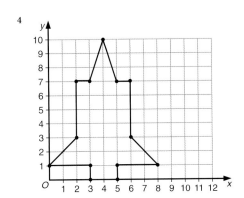

8

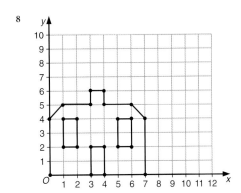

5

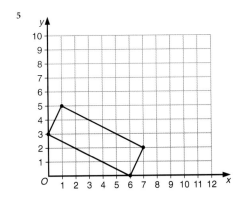

9

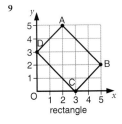

rectangle

10

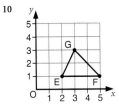

6

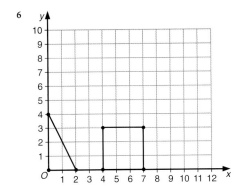

11

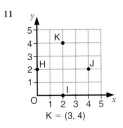

K = (3, 4)

12

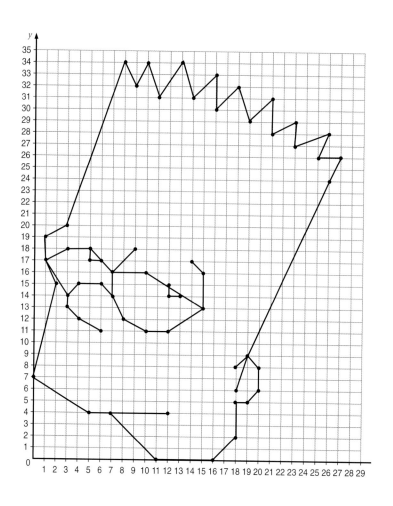

Review exercise 11

1 A(10, 5)   B(1, 4)   C(5, 4)   D(7, 2)   E(3, 0)   F(9, 0)   G(0, 0)

2 **(a)** (0, 5)   **(b)** (4, 10)   **(c)** (10, 0)   **(d)** (2, 0)   **(e)** (6, 3)
   (f) (6, 7)   **(g)** (1, 12)   **(h)** (0, 9)   **(i)** (9, 10)   **(j)** (11, 5)
   (k) (7, 0)   **(l)** (5, 5)   **(m)** (8, 4)

3

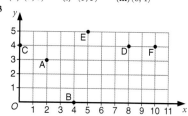

4

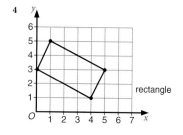

rectangle

5

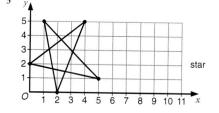

star

6

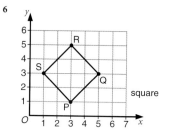

square

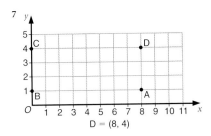

D = (8, 4)

Chapter 12

Exercise 12.1

1

Hex	Tri	Sq	Oct	Pent	Rect
6	3	4	8	5	4

2 (a) square   (b) hexagon   (c) rectangle
  (d) pentagon   (e) octagon   (f) triangle
  (g) hexagon   (h) rectangle   (i) circle
3 (a) triangle   (b) square   (c) rectangle   (d) square
  (e) square   (f) rectangle   (g) rectangle   (h) pentagon
  (i) hexagon   (j) octagon   (k) rectangle   (l) pentagon

Exercise 12.2

1

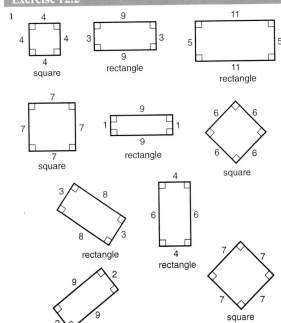

Exercise 12.3

1 (a) scalene   (b) right (scalene)   (c) isosceles (right)
  (d) equilateral   (e) isosceles   (f) right (scalene)
  (g) scalene   (h) isosceles   (i) right (scalene)
2 (a) right (scalene)   (b) isosceles   (c) scalene
  (d) equilateral   (e) isosceles   (f) right (scalene)
3 (a) scalene   (b) right (scalene)   (c) isosceles
  (d) isosceles (right)   (e) isosceles   (f) isosceles

Exercise 12.4

1 (a) triangular prism   (b) cuboid   (c) pentagonal prism
  (d) pyramid   (e) cylinder   (f) cube
  (g) cone   (h) cuboid   (i) cylinder
  (j) pyramid   (k) sphere   (l) triangular

2 (a) cuboid   (b) cylinder   (c) cube
  (d) triangular prism   (e) pentagonal prism   (f) pyramid prism
  (g) sphere   (h) cone   (i) pentagonal prism
3 (a) cubes and cuboids   (b) cuboids and pyramids
  (c) triangular prisms   (d) cubes and cylinders
4 (a) cubes   (b) cubes and pyramids
  (c) cones and cylinders   (d) cubes and spheres

Exercise 12.5

1 (a) vertex   (b) edge   (c) face   (d) edge
  (e) face   (f) vertex   (g) face   (h) vertex
  (i) edge   (j) edge   (k) face   (l) edge

2 (a)

v	8
e	12
f	6

(b)

v	8
e	12
f	6

(c)

v	5
e	8
f	5

(d)

v	6
e	9
f	5

(e)

v	6
e	9
f	5

(f)

v	8
e	12
f	6

(g)

v	4
e	6
f	4

(h)

v	1
e	1
f	2

3 (a) T   (b) F   (c) T   (d) F
  (e) T   (f) F   (g) T   (h) T
  (i) T   (j) T   (k) T

Review exercise 12

1 (a) square   (b) triangle   (c) rectangle   (d) pentagon
2 (a) 3   (b) 4   (c) 6   (d) 5
3 (a) triangle   (b) rectangle   (c) square
4

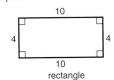

5 (a) isosceles   (b) equilateral   (c) right (scalene)
  (d) scalene   (e) isosceles   (f) right (scalene)
6 (a) right (scalene)   (b) scalene   (c) isosceles
7 (a) cuboid   (b) cube   (c) pyramid   (d) cylinder
8 (a) vertex   (b) edge   (c) face   (d) face
  (e) vertex   (f) face   (g) edge   (h) face
  (i) vertex   (j) face   (k) edge   (l) vertex
9 (a)

v	8
e	12
f	6

v	4
e	6
f	4

10 (a) T   (b) F   (c) T   (d) T   (e) F

Chapter 13

1 (c) 1, 3, 7 and 9; odd numbers
2 (c) in each case: sum of digits = 9
3 (a) (i) 36 (ii) 54 (iii) 9 (iv) 63
  (b) pupils own choice
  (c) All the answers are divisible by 9 (in 9 times table)
4 pupils' drawing
5 pupils' drawing
6 pupils' drawing
7 pupils' drawing
8 pupils' drawing

Index